Out of the Depths:
Sermons and Essays

Kenneth E. Kovacs

Parson's Porch Books

Out of the Depths: Sermons and Essays
ISBN: Softcover 978-1536959758
Copyright © 2016 by Kenneth E. Kovacs

All rights reserved. No part of this book may be reproduced or transmitted in any form or by any means, electronic or mechanical, including photocopying, recording, or by any information storage and retrieval system, without permission in writing from the publisher.

Cover: Jacopo Bassano (1510-1592), "The Miraculous Draught of Fishes" (1545), National Gallery of Art, Washington, DC. (Photo: K.E. Kovacs)

To order additional copies of this book, contact:

Parson's Porch Books
1-423-475-7308
www.parsonsporch.com

Parson's Porch Books is an imprint of Parson's Porch & Company (PP&C) in Cleveland, Tennessee. PP&C is an innovative company which raises money by publishing books of noted authors, representing all genres. All donations from contributors and profits from publishing are shared with the poor.

Out of the Depths:
Sermons and Essays

Table of Contents

Introduction	9
What is God Dreaming Through You?	13
Way Too Literal	20
To See with the Eyes of Love	26
Love the One You're With	31
Presbyterians and Predestination	37
Caring with a Shepherd's Heart	43
Seeking After Jesus	47
Life in the Spirit	53
When Jesus Wept	58
God Gifted	62
Life-Giver	67
Unlocking the Doors of Fear	72
Removing Every Tear	78
Finding Your Way Home	82
A World of Distractions	88
The Call to Listen	94
A Wild, Wondrous Journey	100
Making All Things New	105
Weighed Down with Worry	110
More Truth, More Light	116
Dreaming the Dream Forward	122
Always Reforming	128
The Reconciliation of All Things	135
Sounding Through: On Pastoral Identity	140
Containing the Sacred	144
The Eyes of Experience	148

In memoriam

Reverend Lawson Richard Brown
(1931-2015)

Minister

Mentor

Friend

Introduction

One of my favorite stories is the calling of Simon in Luke 5. They had been out on the Sea of Galilee (or Gennesaret) all night, fishing, and hadn't caught a thing. We often read this text as saying something about discipleship and evangelism and extending the Realm of God. It does have something to say about "catching people" (Luke 5:10).[1] However, before Simon begins this work he has to first do something else.

"Look, Master, we've been out here all night and didn't catch a thing. We're tired. And there are all those people who keep following you around. We just want to go home."

What did Jesus ask him do? "Put out into the deep water and let down your nets for a catch" (Luke 5:4). Put out into the deep water. Let down your nets, into the depths, for a catch. And when they did so they had so many fish that their nets almost began to break. Simon signaled for help. And then both these boats were filled to capacity with fish so that they started to sink under the weight. *Overwhelmed by the abundance of the depths!*

Jesus' invitation to let down our nets into the depths has guided my life for decades. When Jesus tells us to put out into the deep, I can't help but hear this as a summons to go down and in, to enter into the depths of my being, my soul, my heart, my psyche—they're all synonymous for me. The sea is a metaphor for the heart, a symbol of the unconscious, that which lives below the surface of awareness. It's an invitation to go down and in, to an abundance, an overabundant yield that cannot be contained.

When we go down and into the depths, we discover a richness that can't be found when we live on the surface. By going inward, I don't mean being self-focused or egocentric or narcissistic. Just the opposite. In the depths we discover a clearer, truer sense of who we are. I resonate with the psalmist who spoke to God from the deepest recesses of his psyche. "Out of the depths I cry to you, O Lord. Lord hear my voice" (Psalm 130:1). *De profundis*. It's from out of the depths that we experience the pain and anguish, the pain and doubt and fears and anxieties, as well as the joy, love, grace, and the deepest desires of our hearts. From that inner place we cry out to God and relate to God. In the depths we encounter the Abundance who dwells in the dark waters of the soul and calls us to life.

The use of the word *depth* in Luke 5:4, *bathos* in Greek, implies immensity, expansiveness, a spatial depth either of water or earth. It speaks of something

---

[1] All Biblical quotations are from the *New Revised Standard Version*, unless otherwise noted.

profound, fundamental, that which undergirds this world and sustains our lives. In Gnosticism, God is referred to as *bathos*, the depth, the source of all our being. God is not so much "up there," high and lofty, but deep and unfathomable. We find a similar image in the Corinthian correspondence. Paul says that before the Holy Spirit speaks to the human spirit she first searches the "very depths of God." The Spirit reaches from the depths of God to the depths of the human spirit, which means that the words of the Holy Spirit that strike our hearts and move our bodies and shape our lives first move through the depths of God and convey the depths of God to us—from depth to depth. Amazing.

What did Simon Peter do when he saw all that fish? He fell down at Jesus' feet and said, "Go away from me, Lord, for I am a sinful man!" (Luke 5:8). Or, in other words, "Go away from me, Lord, for I'm not worthy of this. Or, "Go away from me, Lord, for I'm not ready for this." Why? "For he and all who were with him were amazed at the catch of fish they had taken;" (Luke 5:9).

If we're honest, we each have a little Simon in us, who when confronted by the power and holiness of God, when faced with awe and amazement before the abundance of God, recoiled and said, "Too much. I can't handle it. I can't withstand it. I can't stand it." And Simon doesn't, literally, because he falls to his knees. It's too much. With God it's always too much. God *is* The Too Much!

Simon said, "Go away from me, Lord. ... " It's a defensive response to the Holy. It's a defense against living in and with and through the amazing claim that God is within us and available to us. When we go into the depths, eventually we will find God. However, I think the knowledge and possibility of the "too much" overwhelms us and scares us, which is why we're reluctant to go there, and why it's easier to live on the surface with a superficial faith or why the Church gets sidetracked in soul-crushing debates or why we simply say to God, "Go away." Perhaps we know that the more we acknowledge what's within, when we become aware of our capacity, when we listen to the divine summons in the depths, the greater the responsibility. We're conflicted, aren't we? We might pray, "Be present in my life, God." But we also hope, "But not too much." We pray, "Speak, God, reveal yourself!" But we don't want to hear anything that's going to cause our boats to sink or overwhelm or what we can't handle or what's going to mess up our world or our value-system, or our career plans, nothing that would elicit that kind of change. And so we keep the Holy at bay, "domesticating transcendence," as William Placher (1948-2008) said, keeping it tame. And we pay a price – in our hearts and in the church, and the world suffers because of it.²

So, what if there is all this abundance in the depths of our souls? Jungian psychoanalyst James Hollis believes there is. "As children we listened to the sound of the sea still echoing in the shell we picked up by the shore. That ancestral roar still links us to the great sea which surges within us as well."³ What if there is "a great sea surging within us"? What if there's all this abundance in our souls: largeness, potential, possibility, love, mercy, generosity, joy? What if it's all there, not on the surface, not in shallow spiritual superficialities, but in the depths, given by the Source, waiting to be caught and shared?

I believe that we encounter God most powerfully in the depths, when we risk going out into the deep water and then letting down our nets. We could almost say that Jesus is calling us to go down—even *grow down*—rather than up. Maybe we need to grow down before we can reach out to others. Paul Tillich (1886-1965) once asked (in a sermon that had an enormous influence upon my life more than thirty years ago), "Why have [people] always asked for truth? Is it because they have been disappointed with the surfaces, and have known that the truth which does not disappoint dwells below the surfaces in the depth?"⁴

The writings of depth psychologist/psychiatrist Carl Gustav Jung (1875-1961) have allowed me to go deeper. Jung has been a companion along my way since my college years, even more so in recent years. Jung was not afraid to encounter the depths of his own unconscious and discovered there an abundance that the psychoanalytic world has yet to fully fathom. Jung has much to say to the contemporary Church and to the discipline of theology. Increasingly, I feel called to help bridge the worlds of depth psychology and theology. Jung's ideas have informed my theology and my preaching (especially over the last ten years) and you'll find evidence of this throughout, both explicitly and implicitly. The last two pieces in the collection are essays written for two Jungian-related publications, the Jung Society of Atlanta and The Zurich Laboratory (www.zurichlab.org).

The sermons in this collection emerged out of the depths of my experience. They were all preached at Catonsville Presbyterian Church, where I've been

---

2 William Placher, *The Domestication of Transcendence: How Modern Thinking about God Went Wrong* (Louisville: Westminster John Knox Press, 1996).
3 James Hollis, *The Archetypal Imagination* (College State: Texas A & M University Press, 2000), 119.
4 Paul Tillich, "The Depth of Existence" in *The Shaking of the Foundations* (New York: Charles Scribner's Sons, 1948), 53.

blessed to serve as pastor since 1999. I pray that both the sermons and essays will speak to a deep place in you. May they help you to go deep(er) into the Abundance in you. And then, may the Holy Spirit reveal the capacity within your life, given to you for the sake of the world and the ongoing reform of the Church.

Together, these sermons and essays are offered here in memory of the Rev. Lawson R. Brown. I was Lawson's assistant minister at St. Leonard's and Cameron Parish Churches, St. Andrews, Scotland from 1990 to 1991. For almost twenty-five years, as both mentor and friend, he supported my ministry, cheered me on when I was feeling discouraged, offered wise counsel, and taught me much about being a servant of the Word.

Kenneth Kovacs

What is God Dreaming Through You?

Genesis 28:10-19a

There's more going on around us than we know. There's more going on within us than we can imagine. That's what Jacob discovered one night in a dream. Jacob the trickster, the fugitive, is running from Esau, his brother; Jacob is running from God, running from himself. Alone. The sun abandoned the day and gave way to night, and in the night Jacob gave way to sleep. He crawled up beside a large stone and slept. Tired. Exhausted. In that place unnamed, Jacob slept. Some place. In this no-place, this non-descript, seemingly godforsaken place, this wilderness place, Jacob was given a dream.

Given a dream. The Dream Maker gifted him with an image of a *ramp* (not really a ladder, but a ramp) that went from the ground and reached up into the heavens. The kind of ramp Jacob no doubt saw in Mesopotamia, ramps built along the four sides of a ziggurat, those terraced temples of Babylon, the top levels of which were known as the "gates of heaven." In the dream the ramp is a busy place, fluid with movement, with messengers of Yahweh moving up and down, conveying the Word of Yahweh, translating between heaven and earth. As Jacob was sleeping, as he was dreaming, Yahweh moved up over him, poised over him as if whispering in Jacob's ear, and Yahweh said, "I, the LORD, am the God of Abraham your father and the God of Isaac. The land on which you lie, to you I will give it and to your seed. And your seed shall be like the dust of the earth and you shall burst forth to the west and the east and the north and the south, and all the clans of the earth shall be blessed through you, and through your seed. And, look, *I am with you and I will guard you wherever you go*, and I will bring you back to this land for I will not leave you until I have done that which I have spoken to you."[1]

Jacob awoke into a new day, into a world transfigured. He remembered the dream and said, "Indeed, the LORD is in this place, and I did not know. How *awesome* is this place? This is the house of God. Here is the gate of heaven." Filled with holy fear, Jacob realized that the encounter in that place brought him up against the *otherness* of the Holy.

In those moments, awe overcomes us as we encounter the Other who is Yahweh. You discover that the land upon which you stand is holy, and you take off your shoes. You bow before the Holiness of the LORD with humility and begin to worship—worship like you've never worshipped before, for you

---

[1] Robert Alter's translation in *The Five Books of Moses: A Translation with Commentary* (New York: W. W. Norton & Company, 2004).

know you're standing at the threshold of the Holy, the sanctuary, the house of the One who holds the universe in love.

This non-place becomes *some* place because in *this* place, and potentially any place, the Holiness of God breaks through. I did not know the LORD was in *this place*. You see, there's more going on around us and within us than we know.

Yahweh is closer than we think or dare to believe. Even though Jacob is running, he can't run from God. Even though Jacob thinks he's in charge of his life, he's actually a pivotal figure in the larger drama of God's plan and promise to provide a land and a future to God's people, and nothing Jacob does—selfish, scheming, swindler that he is—is going to stand in the way of God's promise.

But Jacob is more than just a pawn in God's cosmic scheme. God wants Jacob to know who Jacob is and God wants Jacob to know who *God* really is. God's promise *includes* Jacob; it involves Jacob realizing that the running can stop because his life is of greater meaning than his self-absorbed preoccupations and all the guilt and the fear and the shame of his past. He can let it all go. Jacob's life has cosmic significance. If he would just relax and stop running, he would discover that.

Indeed, Jacob discovered that Yahweh is close. Jacob discovered that Yahweh likes to appear in surprising places, making mundane places *holy*. That's why I'm repeating the word "place" so often, because the text does. The Hebrew word for "place" here, *hamaqom*, later came to be a name for God in post-biblical times. Rabbis said that God is to be understood as *place*, understood as *place* that encompasses the world.[2] And so any place has the potential of becoming the place where we encounter the Holy One. God is not limited to sanctuaries or temples or churches.

Celtic Christians believed that there are places in the world, such as Iona off the coast of Scotland, *thin* places where there seems to be a permeable membrane separating heaven and earth, places where one feels really close to God. You know something *other* is there, another world is close. I've felt this myself several times in Iona.

Any place can be the place where we encounter the holy. I sometimes think the inside of a CT-scan or MRI machine must be one of the holiest places in our world. Think of all the prayer that is offered in those places, people asking

---

[2] Taken from *The Torah: A Modern Commentary*, ed. W. Gunther Plaut (NY: Union of American Hebrew Congregations, 1981). One rabbi said: "God is the place of the world, but the world is not His place."

for and experiencing God's presence there. Think of a garbage dump outside the walls of Jerusalem—otherwise known as Golgotha—a place of execution that became the place where the glory of God's suffering love was revealed on a cross. If God can be present there, then God can be anywhere. What about a drug and rat-infested row house in West Baltimore or a slum in Kinshasa?

There's more going on around us than we know or can even imagine. We have to be open to it. We have to pray that our hearts and ears and eyes are open to God's presence. When you do, you'll meet God in very surprising places.

But if you're the skeptical or logical type, the type that only sees what you want to see, believes only what you want to believe, if you like to be in control, if there's a Jacob in you, maybe running from God, running from yourself, then don't be surprised if God meets you in precisely those places where you're *not* in control, where your ego-defenses are down—as when you're asleep, when you *dream*.

Just as there are geographical places that convey the Holy, that allow us to engage in heaven-to-earth, human-divine conversations, it is significant that scripture tells us there are internal, psychic places that are like those ramps, where heaven and earth converse, where we receive a divine word of promise and hope and assurance that directs our steps and waking moments. A dream is like a ramp between two worlds, between the unconscious and the conscious. But a dream, scripture tells us, can also be a ramp between heaven and earth, between the human and divine.

It is not surprising that Sigmund Freud (1856-1939), shaped as he was by his own Jewish experience, would put so much stock in the importance of dreams. His collection of essays, *The Interpretation of Dreams* (1900), was a bombshell upon the moral, prudishness of Victorian Europe, and one of the great pieces of Western literature.[3] Of course, Freud had problems with the notion of God, but he showed us the power of the unconscious to shape our waking moments. Freud's colleague and close friend, Carl Jung eventually separated from Freud and severed their relationship, in part because Jung wanted to embrace the psychological importance of the God-experience, whereas Freud was suspicious of Jung's interests.[4] Freud basically believed

---

[3] First published in 1900, with the German title, *Die Traumdeutung*, which could be translated, "Dream meanings."
[4] See Jung's biography, *Memories, Dreams, Reflections*, recorded and edited by Aniela Jaffé; translated from the German by Richard and Clara Winston (New York: Vintage Books, 1971), in which he vividly tells his separation from Freud, including accounts of Freud fainting when

that the unconscious was like a trash compactor and that dreams helped to "process" the events of waking life. Jung, on the other hand, saw the unconscious as a vast source of wisdom. It's claimed that 90% of who we are is unconscious, leaving 10% for consciousness; like an iceberg, we see only the tip. The wisdom of that other 90% is conveyed to us through our dreams. Son of a Reformed pastor in Switzerland, Jung said that in our time, "We have forgotten the age-old fact that God speaks chiefly through dreams and visions."[5] If you want to know where God might still be speaking today, pay attention to your dreams.

Now, to be clear, *not* every dream is from God (thank God!), but every dream has meaning, multiple meanings and is given to us as sheer gift for the purpose of health and wholeness. No dream is given just to tell us what we already know, but something we need to know for our wellbeing, to move us along life's way.

Jung was only reclaiming something that Jacob knew: *God speaks to us through our dream life.* Everyone dreams, every night, whether you remember your dreams or not. You dream. Time and again the importance of dreams surface in the Bible. They're still important. But unless we're in analysis or know how to listen to them, we generally don't take our dreams seriously or see them as companions on our walk with God.

Genesis 37:5 tells us, "Joseph dreamed a dream, and he told it to his brothers and they hated him yet the more."[6] Perhaps that's your experience with dreams. Maybe you discount them. How often have we heard it said, or maybe you say it yourself, "It's only a dream" or "It's just a dream." Just. Just. Just. Such a "soul-crushing word."[7]

Dreams are more than "just" dreams—they have immense power, and when used by God, they have extraordinary power to redeem and help make us whole. For more than twenty-five years now I have kept track of my dreams, giving greater attention to them over the last seven to ten years, in particular. I write them down in the middle of the night. I have a pen and pad beside my bed, and I write down (sometimes in the dark) what I remember. I work with them daily. I listen to them. I amplify them. I don't try to interpret them.

---

the subject of God came up in conversations (146ff). See also Jung's Terry Lectures delivered at Yale University, *Psychology and Religion.* (New Haven: Yale University Press, 1938).
[5] C. G. Jung, *Man and His Symbols* (1953). See also C. G. Jung, *Dream Interpretation Ancient and Modern: Notes from the Seminar Given in 1936-1941*, edited by John Peck, Lorenz Jung, and Maria Meyer-Grass (Princeton: Princeton University Press, 2014).
[6] Robert Alter's translation.
[7] There's a scene in the movie *Finding Neverland* (Miramax, 2004) about the life of J. M. Barrie (1860-1937), the author of *Peter Pan*, in which Barrie scorns the use of the word, "just"—as "such a soul-crushing word."

I live with them. Over the years I have had three or four in which I know beyond a doubt God was speaking to me. They were significant, life-changing dreams that pointed me in a particular direction, and they continue to shape me today. There's more going on around us than we know. There's more going on within us than we know or imagine.

Maybe you're still skeptical. That's okay. Here's a story from the last time I preached on this text, back in 2005. During my time preparing for the sermon that week, I came across an interview with the South African novelist and travel writer, Laurens van der Post (1906-1996); one of his books became the film, *The Lost World of the Kalahari*, produced by the BBC in 1956. I was familiar with the name but didn't know much about him. In the interview, he talked about growing up in the Calvinist world of South Africa where he read the Bible and was fascinated by the importance of dreams. He later met Carl Jung, in 1949, whose own Calvinist background and psychological underpinnings allowed them to become fast friends. Van der Post believed, "a dream is the instrument of creative change."[8] In an interview with the Bushman, one hunter said to him, "There's a dream dreaming us." When pressed to explain, the hunter was moved by what he said and simply replied, "I can't tell you more, but there's a dream dreaming us."[9] That stayed with me all week.

Then, on the Saturday of that week, I was roaming through a used bookstore in Washington, DC, on Connecticut Avenue, glancing over some books in the religion section, when my eyes rested on the spine of a book. I was drawn to one book in particular with large letters that read JUNG. Because of my considerable interest in Jung, I pulled it from the shelf. I looked at the cover and discovered that it was written by Laurens van der Post! I bought it, grabbed some coffee, and sat down to read. In the first couple of pages van der Post talked about the importance of dreams. Then I discovered that he devoted two full pages to Jacob's ladder or ramp dream, which he called, "the greatest of all dreams ever dreamt."[10] Now, Jung wouldn't call my experience a coincidence, but an example of synchronicity. (Jung was the first to describe synchronicity.[11]) It's essentially a message of the psyche: *pay attention to this, Kenneth, this is important.*

---

[8] Laurens van der Post, "Dialogues with Sir Laurens van der Post," New Dimension Tapes, http://www.newdimensions.org/online-journal/articles/singular-individual.html
[9] "Dialogues."
[10] Laurens van der Post, *Jung & the Story of Our Time* (New York: Pantheon Books, 1975), 12. Jacob's dream "remains," he said, "the greatest of all dreams ever dreamt and the progenitor of all the other dreams, visionary material, and mythological and allegorical activity that were to follow" in the Bible.
[11] See C. G. Jung, "Synchronicity: An Acausal Connecting Principle," *The Collected Works of C. G. Jung*, Vol. 8 (Princeton: Princeton University Press, 1970).

So I drove back to Baltimore, to Dickeyville, and was about to sit down to write the sermon around 6:00 p.m. (Now, I usually don't wait until Saturday evenings to write the sermon each week. Some weeks I sense resistance within me, and I put it off because it's not ready to be written.) So, it was Saturday evening, in Dickeyville, when—poof—the power went out. A fire truck spun out of control on North Forest Park and hit a utility pole (thankfully, the firemen were okay). Frustrated, I packed up my things and headed for the Church House to write the sermon. I turned on the computer, prayed, waited for the computer to fire up, and stared out the window behind the monitor, facing north, when my eyes focused on what had been staring at me for weeks, but I never really noticed it: a tree, with a ladder leaning up against it. But on that Saturday evening the ladder was placed lower down on the tree, making the ladder look more like a *ramp*. The ladder. The ramp. The way of moving between two worlds. I can see that ladder and the tree in my mind's eye. The ladder seemed to shimmer, as though illuminated. It wasn't actually glowing, but that's how it felt. Synchronicity again. I got it and I laughed out loud: *this is important, pay attention, Kenneth.*

There is so much more going on around us than we can imagine. There is so much more going on within us than we know. Our world is connected to another world, and that other world, so very close, as close as our dreams, is the source of life and grants meaning to our lives. What matters most in the life of faith is making that connection. The closing words of E. M. Forster's (1879-1970), *Howard's End*, says it all: "Only connect."[12] *Only connect*. What matters most is the connection, the fluid movement between heaven and earth, up and down on that ramp. I think van der Post gets to the heart of what Jacob discovered in his dream: "No matter how abandoned and without help either in themselves or the world about them, men [and women] are never alone because that which, acknowledged or unacknowledged, dreams through them is always *by* their side."[13] By their side. And I would add, as I have learned, the one who dreams through us is also *on* our side. On our side.

The one who dreams through us is God. This is a bold claim, I know, but the text leads us to such conclusions. My own experience backs it up. Jacob didn't have to ask for help; it just came. It was gift—sheer *grace*. He didn't *have* a dream, the dream had him; it was given to him. And the dream spoke so clearly to his situation—telling him that his life is worthy of God's divine protection and promise—"I am with you and I will guard you wherever you go." The dream grants a future, grants him a *telos*. He didn't have to worry

---

[12] E. M. Forster, *Howard's End* (1910), "Only connect! That was the whole of her sermon. Only connect the prose and the passion, and both will be exalted, and human love will be seen at its height. Live in fragments no longer. Only connect, and the beast and the monk, robbed of the isolation that is life to either, will die." (Chapter 22).
[13] Van der Post, p. 12.

about his future. When Jacob realized this, it provided him with the assurance he needed to fulfill the meaning and purpose of his life.[14]

Then Jacob did what you would do: he began to worship, *really worship* Yahweh. And he set up a reminder, established a shrine, so that he would never, ever forget what he learned in that dream.

So, what is God dreaming through you?

---

[14] Van der Post, "For Jacob had not even to ask for help from beyond himself. The necessities of his being had spoken so eloquently from him that the dream brought him instant promise of help from that which had created him, henceforth to the end of his days, and of those who were to follow in his way after him." (12).

Way Too Literal

John 6:51-58

Let's stay close to three verses in order to track the conversation between Jesus and his hearers here in John 6. The exchange is a good example of something that has plagued religious life for a very long time, perhaps even more so today.

Here we go. The Revised Common Lectionary over the summer has been walking us through John 6. Our reading today, starting at verse 51, enters a conversation that began earlier in the chapter, when Jesus refers to himself as the "bread of life" (John 6:35). He compares himself to manna, to the bread given by God to Israel during their sojourn in the wilderness. All those that ate manna in the wilderness eventually died. By contrast, Jesus says, "This is the bread that comes down from heaven, so that one may eat of it and not die" (John 6:50). This, then, leads us to verses 51, 52, and 53.

Jesus says, "I am the living bread that came down from heaven. Whoever eats of this bread will live forever; and the bread that I will give for the life of the world is my flesh" (v. 51). "The Jews," that is, the religious leaders listening in on Jesus, begin to quarrel among themselves and then ask, "How can this man give us his flesh to eat?" (v. 52). They're perplexed, confused, probably scandalized. "So Jesus said to them, 'Very truly, I tell you, unless you eat the flesh of the Son of Man and drink his blood, you have no life in him'" (v. 53).

There we have it. Three verses. Jesus speaks. The religious leaders respond. And then Jesus speaks again. But pay close attention to what's happening here, particularly verses 51 and 52. Jesus' statement about being "living bread" and their perplexed response is significant. These two verses, the exchange between them—focus here, zoom in here. They seem to be talking past each other. Jesus is trying to get a message across to them, trying to teach them something, show them something, but they don't get it, they can't hear it. Why is this?

Being the consummate teacher, the rabbi, Jesus offers them a metaphor (bread as flesh/flesh as bread) to help them discover something of God's mission in his life. He uses a metaphor to reveal the truth. But the religious leaders don't understand. Why not? Because they're being literal. As religious leaders they should have been more familiar with metaphor, how it works, how it helps to convey truth. Instead, they respond the way many religious people do, then as now, by being too literal. And it's because they're being too literal that they miss the message. They couldn't hear it. And then they become angry and begin to quarrel amongst themselves. This, too, is often what happens when we're being too literal, especially in the world of religion and spirituality; we become frustrated.

Literalism often hinders us from encountering truth; in fact, literalism is one of the besetting sins of our day. That's how Owen Barfield put it (1898-1997). English solicitor, non-academic philosopher, and devoted Christian, Barfield wrote an enormously important book titled *Saving the Appearances: A Study of Idolatry*, published in 1965 and heralded as one of the top one hundred spiritual works of the twentieth-century. Barfield said, "The besetting sin today is the sin of literalism."[1] Barfield was a close friend of C. S. Lewis (1898-1963). Lewis penned *The Lion, The Witch, and the Wardrobe* for Owen's daughter, Lucy; he wrote *The Voyage of the Dawn Treader* for Owen's son, Geoffrey. These are stories, as we know, full of metaphors.

Before we explore why it's a sin, I should probably say what we mean by literalism. Literalism is the belief, the philosophy, the attitude, the assumption that truth can *only* be found in exactness and certainty. It's an obsession (and it can be an obsession) with what is actual, *literal*, with the "letter of the law," with the need to nail down (sometimes, actually) what is true and not true and then defending that "truth" at all costs. Literalism is a way of being and believing that seeks to maintain a tight "hold" on reality. It's a way of being that is suspicious (perhaps paranoid) of anything that smacks of analogy or metaphor, of anything that leaves open the possibility of multiple meanings, of plurality. For the literalist there can only be *one* interpretation of a text, whether sacred (such as the Koran or the Bible) or secular (such as the U. S. Constitution), only *one* meaning, only *one* way to believe and *one* way to be in the world. The literalist will take a metaphor and try to turn it into a thing, an idea, a historic *fact*. Or, a literalist fails to understand the meaning of a metaphor because s/he is, well, a literalist.

What's wrong with this? Why is literalism a sin? There are times when a person needs to be very literal and factual and exact and concrete, especially if they're an engineer designing a bridge or an airplane. We all want our engineers to be literal and concrete.

But when it comes to the world of religion and spirituality, when it comes to God as subject, when it comes to the message of the gospel, when it comes to the world of the Bible, which is shot through with metaphor and symbol, if we approach the text and the story too literally we might then miss the

---

[1] Owen Barfield, *Saving the Appearances: A Study of Idolatry* (Wesleyan, 1988).

message. And this is why it's a kind of sin because literalism separates us from the truth, separates us from the gospel, and separates us from God.

Literalism hardens our hearts and impedes our imaginations from encountering God's mystery in the world.[2] It prevents us from approaching mystery. It narrows by making the multiple into one; multiple meanings, multiple definitions, and multiple interpretations are reduced to one, monolithic meaning. Literalism abhors the symbolic, the metaphoric, the "as-if" quality of words, of truth, of experience. Literalism, when taken to its extreme, leads to fundamentalisms of all varieties, also associated with texts, with words and the meaning of words. We see this particularly in religion, in fights over how the Bible or the Koran may be interpreted, which then leads to conflicts over ethics, morality, and competing worldviews.

A contemporary of Barfield who also warned about the dangers of literalism was Norman O. Brown (1913-2000). Scholar and classicist, Brown wrote, "The thing to be abolished is literalism." And, as Brown insisted, the "alternative to literalism is mystery."[3] In our age we often assume that if we have a literal meaning of something, then we know more about it, the truth of what something really is. Sometimes people say that something is "just" or "only" a symbol or "just" or "only" a metaphor, dismissing their power to convey the truth. However, ironically, an obsession with the literal actually blocks what can be known and obstructs our relation to mystery, and thus hinders the possibility of discovering what can be known. As a result, a lot of the truth contained in the Bible is completely missed because people read it literally, instead of metaphorically or symbolically.

James Hollis, a Jungian analyst and writer, reminds us, "The sacred is only knowable through experience and then made meaningful and communicated by the agencies of metaphor and symbol."[4] "Symbol," from the Greek, *symbolon*, means to throw together. Ideas, images are thrown together into a symbol and a symbol has power because it then points to something else, something beyond it, which gives it meaning. Think of the cross as symbol. "Metaphor," from the Greek *metaphora* means to carry over, to bear, to transfer meaning from one place to the other.

---

[2] James Hillman, *Re-Visioning Psychology* (Harper & Row, 1975), 149: "Literalism prevents mystery by narrowing the multiple ambiguity of meanings into one definition. Literalism is the natural concomitant of monotheistic consciousness—whether in theology or science—which demands singleness of meaning."
[3] Norman O. Brown in a response to Herbert Marcuse (1898-1979) in his *Negations* (London, 1968), cited in Hillman, 149.
[4] James Hollis, *The Archetypal Imagination* (College Station, TX: Texas A & M University Press, 2000), 42.

Isn't this what Jesus is doing with all of these references to bread? Jesus uses a metaphor to make a spiritual claim to help move his hearers from one understanding of himself to another. The metaphor carries us, bears us, and transfers us deeper into our understanding of Jesus. Without the metaphor we take Jesus literally and then think we have to become cannibals in order to follow him, which completely misses the point. Metaphor allows us to go deep, to have a more profound meaning of something, to discover what is not obviously available on the surface. In many ways, Jesus is an enormous metaphor who carries and transfers meaning from God to all of us.

It's easy (I think) to see why literalism is so dangerous and why the world and the Church are suffering, terribly, from it. The literalist bent undergirds and stands behind the many expressions of fundamentalism (religious and otherwise) unleashing its toxic effluence throughout the public square and the Church. The unmitigated fact is that reality is infinitely more complicated and complex than fundamentalists will acknowledge, actually more than they are free to admit. Literalism and fundamentalism are a form of bondage, the opposite of freedom; they are defensive reactions against the ever-increasing intricacies and challenges of the contemporary world. Fundamentalism and its bedfellow literalism have inflicted untold damage upon the world of religious faith, the very faith they say they care most about and try to defend and preserve.

So what do we do? How do we reclaim the importance of metaphor and symbol? How do we move away from literalist readings of a text? Perhaps we should first deal with the assumption that the Bible is a book of history, always giving a factual account of what actually happened in the past. Yes, the Bible has to do with historical periods and people who really lived in history. However, the writers of the Bible were not trying to give us historical accounts of what *actually* took place. They were trying to tell a story about God, about the world, about redemption, about hope.

The contemporary New Testament scholar John Dominic Crossan summed up the purpose of his life work in this way: "My point is not that those ancient people told literal stories and we are now smart enough to take them symbolically, but that they told them symbolically and we are now dumb enough to take them literally. They knew what they were doing; we don't."[5]

Northrop Frye (1912-1999), the literary critic and theorist, one of the towering intellectuals of the twentieth century, said, "When the Bible is historically accurate, it is only accidentally so: reporting was not of the

---

[5] John Dominic Cross, *Who is Jesus?* (Louisville: Westminster John Knox Press, 2007) 31, cited in Tacey, *Religion as Metaphor: Beyond Literal Belief* (New Brunswick, NJ: Transaction Publishers, 2015), 16.

slightest interest to its writers. They had a story to tell which could only be told by myth and metaphor: what they wrote became a source of vision rather than doctrine. The Bible is, with unimportant exceptions, written in the literary language of myth and metaphor."[6]

Metaphor is one of the ways we get to the truth; it helps to carry us there. When we read the Bible literally we've ventured over into idolatry, as David Tacey would say. "Literalism engenders idolatry and aggression and is the bane of civilization."[7]

Literalism is a serious threat to the health and vitality of the Church, of Christianity itself. James Hollis suggests that literalism is actually a form of religious blasphemy because it seeks to concretize (nail down, define) and absolutize the core experience of the Holy, of God—a God (if God) who cannot be controlled or defined, a God who remains ultimately a mystery. And a mystery, it's worth saying (again and again!), is not the same as a puzzle (which can be solved); a mystery is *always* enigmatic and is therefore inherently *unknowable*. A mystery cannot be solved and always remains a mystery. We should not try to solve a mystery; instead, we kneel before it and bow and allow the truth of the encounter to shape us.

Humility of knowledge is essential whenever we attempt to make truth claims. Thinking we comprehend the truth is a fantasy. I'm not saying the truth doesn't exist or that it's completely inaccessible; it just means we need to remember that our "hold" on it is always elusive.

Hollis—a friend whose insight and wisdom I respect enormously—even argues that literalism is a kind of psychopathology in need of deep healing (redemption?). Is it a personality disorder? From his many years as a psychoanalyst, he has come to see that a way to gauge mental health and emotional maturity is the degree to which one is able to tolerate what he calls the triple A's: ambiguity, ambivalence, and anxiety.[8] The ability to hold these in tension—and not escape into literalism and fundamentalism and other strategies of avoidance (such as addiction)—is a way to test one's psychic strength. I can certainly resonate with this. The literalists (of all varieties) I have known and know—and love—and who at times drive me crazy have difficulty tolerating ambiguity, ambivalence, and anxiety—and sometimes for *very* good reasons. However, they use their faith or relationship to a text or their political ideology to bolster themselves against, protect their fearful egos

---

[6] Northrop Frye, *Words with Power* (Ontario: Viking, 1990), xiv, cited in Tacey, 17.
[7] Tacey, xi.
[8] Hollis, 63.

from, hide themselves from ambiguity, ambivalence, and anxiety that define the human condition.

So what do we do? As with every sin, confession is good for the soul. Forgiveness and healing are possible. Perhaps counseling and therapy are also in order. This struggle is real and serious. The pushback from literalists is strong. Several years ago I wrote a short article about the threats of literalism, and I became the topic of several fundamentalist websites that took me to task.

Jesus offers us bread; he offers himself *as* bread. He offers us a metaphor. He gave us so many metaphors of himself. We're invited to play with them, imaginatively engage them, hold them gently, and not take them literally. Metaphor is a gift, given to help us relate to Jesus, fathom the meaning of his life, his message, given so that we can better digest what he has to show us and teach us and show us about the mystery that is God—not to categorically define Jesus or nail him down. How we love to crucify our metaphors. "Very truly, I tell you, unless you eat the flesh of the Son of Man and drink his drink, you have no life in him" (John 6:53). So let us take and eat and drink.

To See with the Eyes of Love

Matthew 5:38-48

What do we do with a text like this? These are demanding words from Jesus—perhaps the most challenging and radical statements in the Sermon on the Mount. You know them well. Go the extra mile. Turn the other cheek. Do not resist the evildoer. Love your neighbor—including your enemy. Be perfect. Be perfect? One has to be perfect just to live up to Jesus' expectations. Are they even realistic?

What do we do with texts like these? We can ignore them, of course (not recommended). We can try to ethically strive to live up to this standard, knowing in advance we will probably fail (miserably). But they're still worthy of our emulation.

I wonder if there isn't another option, one that has less to do with human striving and more to with increasing our capacity to live from within the love of God, like Jesus himself.

These verses are part of the Great Anti-thesis sayings of Jesus. Here, Jesus begins with a quote from the ancient Hammurabi Code, the Babylonian law code that dates back to 1700 BC, "You have heard that it was said, 'An eye for an eye.'" This was the ancient code of justice. A similar ethic is found in the Jewish Law, as well as in Islam. To take another's eye requires an appropriate compensation. To be wronged by another means the scales of justice, equally weighed when justice is served, become weighted. Justice "righted" entails correcting the imbalance. If you steal my cow, I get to steal your cow—and then we're even. Punch me in the face, I get to punch you in the face—then we'll be even.

Justice then, and for many still, means little more than getting even for an offense. This understanding is reflected in our legal language today. We speak of *lex talionis; talion* meaning offense. We often hear that punishment has to equal the crime in order for justice to be served. This might be the way the world operates, but we're not called to be of the world—in the world, but not of it. *In* the world, with a different ethic, a different outlook, a different approach, a different way, a different truth, a different life. As Martin Luther King, Jr. (1929-1968) said, "The old law of an eye for an eye leaves everyone blind."

Jesus says, "But I say to you..." The Great-Anthesis. The contrary view of the gospel. The contravening of grace that provides a "still more excellent way" (1 Cor. 13). And so we have these illustrations —do not resist the evildoer. If someone strikes your right cheek, offer the left; if someone wants to sue the shirt off your back, give him your coat as well; go the extra mile. Give to everyone who begs for you; lend, lend, lend. Now these statements are not what they appear to be. Throughout the history of Christianity, they've been taken literally and have inflicted considerable damage, if not abuse. Some have said that Jesus expects his followers to be passive, to be doormats, suffering through hurt and injustice, never fighting back. These verses have been thrown at women, in particular, by men who expect subservience. Actually, Jesus is not calling for subservience here or passivity. They're actually far more active and engaging than we might think. We could dwell on these verses alone, but the lectionary calls us on to the rest of the chapter.

Similarly, Jesus says, "You have heard that is was said, 'You shall love your neighbor and hate your enemy.'" Now, the Old Testament never says, "hate your enemy." It does say something about loving your neighbor, which then led to the question—but who is my neighbor? The logic went something like this. Yes, Torah, the Law tells me I am to love my neighbor. But if I determine who is not my neighbor—if I define the limits of what constitutes "neighbor," then *that* person is my enemy and I'll be free to hate him or her, without violating the Jewish Law because he is, by definition, not my neighbor. Sure, I can love my neighbor. But those filthy Samaritans and those godless Gentiles, the Law does not apply to them because they're not my neighbors, so I can hate them. Do you see their logic?

Jesus says, "But I say to you ..." Here again, an anti-thesis, the gospel as contrary, the contravening of grace that sets the follower of Jesus off in an entirely different direction, with a different way, a different outlook, a different logic—the unsettling logic of love. "Love your enemies and pray for those who persecute you." Jesus turns the Law on its head. He undermines the prevailing false logic of love reserved only for "neighbors." Grace contravenes—breaks, flouts, disobeys, and even violates the normal way of doing things. Love your enemies—not just accept them, not just put up with them, not just tolerate them, but *love* them. And even—to go an extra mile—pray for the very one who persecutes you.

Why does Jesus set the standard so high, so difficult? It's tough to say, of course, but if the text is the clue it just might have to do with the nature of love itself. We must remember as we hear the Sermon on the Mount, as we receive Jesus' teaching here, that his teaching is always connected to his identity as the Son of God. What he encourages and models for us is an expression, an extension of who he is. When we see Jesus, we see right to the depths of the very heart of God. So that when Jesus calls us to love our enemies, he's inviting us to see that this is the exactly the way God is toward us, pure love. If we are really children of God, then *be* children of God and act the way God does. This is the way God relates to all of us, who are, it must be acknowledged at various times in our lives, enemies of God—enemies, in that we reject God's will, that we do not work for the vision of the kingdom, that we hinder the mission of God, that we fail to love our neighbor and ourselves and even God. In this sense we are "enemies" of God's intentions for the world. There are even times when God and the church are persecuted by forces, ideas, attitudes that also undermine God's intentions for the world.

And how does God act? "For [God] makes his sun rise on the evil and on the good, and sends rain on the righteous and on the unrighteous." God's love does not discriminate. God's love is poured out on all—whether they know it or not, whether they believe in God or not. If you only love those who love you, there's nothing noble or even God-like in that—you're no better than tax collectors (who weren't thought of kindly in Jesus' day, particularly when the Roman Empire was overburdening them with taxes). If you only love people like you, in your family, in your tribe, in your town, who share your ideas and perspectives and faith, there's nothing noble or even God-like in that. Even the Gentiles—who didn't have the reputation among the Jews for being the most ethical people in the world—do a far better job.

Then Jesus throws out a line that causes even more anxiety than the command to love one's enemy and to turn the other cheek: *be perfect*. This command, too, is often misunderstood. It does *not* mean be morally perfect. It does *not* mean be always right. It doesn't mean never make a mistake. It doesn't mean we always have to get an A+ on moral purity. These are all moralistic readings of this text that probably say more about *our* assumptions about the life of faith, than about the text. These are all misreadings of the text.

I really wish the translators of the NRSV (the best translation by-far, the version we have in the pews), offered a better translation here. The New International Version renders it a little better, because it does not use the word "perfect," "But you must always act like your Father in heaven." But it misses the meaning of the Greek word that is poorly translated into English as "perfect." It's the Greek word, *teleos*—meaning *end* or *purpose*. In other words, fulfill your purpose, your end, the reason you exist, just as your heavenly Father acts from within God's purpose, end, from out of his core identity – which is love. Eugene Peterson's version in *The Message* does a better job capturing what's behind the Greek. Peterson translates 5:48 this way: "In a word, what I'm saying is, Grow up. You are kingdom subjects.

Now live like it. Live out your God-created identity. Live generously and graciously toward others, the way God lives toward you."

That's the point: the way God lives toward you—in love—is the way God calls us to live toward others, even our enemies. By love we don't mean romantic love, nor do we mean a kind of passive acceptance; it's not a sentimental feeling toward someone. God's love is not preference. Love is more than preference, to prefer one over the other. That's not love either. Love is not a synonym for "like"—Jesus didn't say, *like* your enemies, but to *love* them. God doesn't just like us, but loves us.

This love is strong. It is powerful. As the Mexican priest says in Graham Greene's (1904-1991) novel, *The Power and the Glory*, God's love is often unrecognizable. "It might even look like hate, it would be enough to scare us—God's love. It set fire to a bush in the desert, didn't it, and smashed open graves and set the dead walking in the dark."[1] It's unsettling. It's disturbing. It's not what we expect.

It's a love that calls people to life and speaks into death itself and forces it to yield life, to yield resurrection. Everyone is worthy of being an object of this love, including our enemies. Perhaps through the eyes of love we might even come to see that the enemy is not an enemy at all. Maybe the one we considered an enemy is someone else altogether. Perhaps when we see the world through the eyes of love, with something of the way God looks out at each of us and the world through the "eyes" of love, then what we're looking at comes into focus. We might discover the enemy is not an enemy—and while maybe not yet a friend—he or she is at least a person, a human being suffering and hungering for life as much as the rest of us.

It was James Loder (1931-2001), one of my professors at Princeton Seminary and one of the wisest persons I've ever known, who showed me what love looks like. He put it this way. Love is "the non-possessive delight in the particularity of the other."[2] Love sees the *other* and does not confuse itself with the other. Love allows the other to exist in freedom and creates a space for the other to be. Love does not try to possess the other, control, define or delimit the other. Love transforms the other from an *it* (an object to be controlled) into a *thou* (a subject who is honored, worthy of respect). Love allows the other to be, to exist apart from oneself, to have a life apart from oneself, and takes immense delight and joy in the particularity, the uniqueness, the incomparability of the other.[3]

---

[1] Graham Greene, *The Power and the Glory* (New York: Penguin Books, 1990 [1940]), 199-200.
[2] James E. Loder, *The Logic of the Spirit: Human Development in Theological Perspective* (San Francisco: Jossey-Bass, 1998), 266-267.
[3] On "particularity" in Loder and the "heightening of particularity" in love, see *The Transforming Moment*, 2nd edition (Colorado Springs: Helmers & Howard, 1989), 198.

To be on the receiving end of such a love as someone else's *other*—to be seen as another's *thou*—we are brought to life and allowed to thrive. To see that this is the way God loves us, as the *thou* of God, we are brought to life and allowed to thrive. Love "earnestly desires the fulfillment of the unique particularity of the other one."[4] This is what we experience when we're in relationship with God and from this dynamic, the vitality of this relationship we turn out toward the people we meet, our enemies, our friends, strangers, whoever stands with us under the rain shower of God's grace.

Love, if it is love, cannot be an ethical duty; neither can it be attained through the efforts of the human spirit. The human capacity to give and receive love is given by participating in a loving relationship with God who is love (1 John 4:7). The command to love would be oppressive if it were not for the fact that God gives the human spirit the ability to love in the intimacy of the Spirit.[5]

God gives us the capacity to love as God loves. To see the world as God sees it. Recently, a colleague introduced me to the poetry of Kathleen Raine (1908-2003). A child of the manse in Scotland, she lived most of her life in Northumbria, where England crosses over into Scotland. She was also known for her scholarship on William Blake (1757-1827). I think she expresses the exquisite wisdom of what Jesus is trying to say here: "Unless you see a thing in the light of love, you do not see a thing at all."[6]

Try putting this into practice this week. Imagine you're looking out upon the world through the lens of love with the hope of really seeing a thing or a person—the people you meet, your coworkers, your children, your partner, your husband, wife, the person sitting beside you, strangers, people that bother you, people who scare you, people you hate, disagree with, try it with your pet, a flower, the moon, the sun, even the rain and, yes, even the snow.

That would be how to love even as God loves us, God loves the world. "Unless you see a thing in the light of love, you do not see a thing at all."

---

[4] *Logic of the Spirit*, 267.
[5] Kenneth E. Kovacs, *The Relational Theology of James E. Loder: Encounter and Conviction* (New York: Peter Lang, 2011).
[6] I'm grateful to Melanie Starr Costello for introducing me to Raine's poetry. This quote is cited in John O'Donohue's (1956-2008), *Anam Cara: A Book of Celtic Wisdom* (HarperCollins, 1989), 65.

Love the One You're With

Psalm 86 & Romans 13:8-10

Several Sundays ago I preached on the parable of the Good Samaritan in Luke 10. Jesus offered this parable in response to the test question posed by the lawyer, "Teacher, what must I do to inherit eternal life?" Jesus responded, "What is written in the law?" The lawyer responded, "You shall love the Lord your God with all your heart, and with all your soul, and with all your strength, and with all your mind; and your neighbor as yourself" (Luke 10:27). The focus of the parable is on the neighbor.

In the response to that sermon, several questions emerged. Love of God: We know something about that, although we're not very good at it. Love for neighbor: We know something more about that, although we're not very good at that either. *But what does it mean to love yourself?* What does this look like? It's clear that the ability to love one's neighbor is inextricably linked to the ability to love one's self. *But how does one love one's self without being or becoming selfish?* And so today's sermon is an attempt to respond to these questions because they're critical ones. Our response will shape the way we understand the Christian life. So with apologies to Crosby, Stills, Nash, and Young, *how do you love the one you're with?* "One" here meaning *oneself*, this *one*, this self within, who we are. *How do we love ourselves?*

These aren't academic questions or abstract curiosities. Pastors confront these issues all the time in ministry because somehow, somewhere along the way people have come to believe that to love one's self is un-Christian, that the love of and care for one's self is actually a sin. What is worse—and I've seen this a lot in my ministry—there are some who even operate with the twisted assumption that as Christians we are supposed to hate and even loathe ourselves, that we are to remove any trace of the self. This is due, in part, to a warped hearing of texts like this one, "If any want to be my followers, let them deny themselves and take up their cross daily and follow me. For those who want to save their life will lose it, and those who lose their life for my sake will save it" (Luke 9:23-24). A misreading of this text has caused considerable damage to the psyche of countless Christians for centuries.

So what does it mean to love one's self? The idea of loving one's self might sound odd. We know something about what it's like to love a spouse or partner, child or grandchild, to love our country or love a pet. But love toward self, this might trip us up. Perhaps using the word *love* is an obstacle. So what if we use other words, such as: *like, value, forgive, kindness, cherish, honor, acceptance*.

What does it mean to like one's self? Value one's self? Forgive one's self? Cherish and honor one's self? What does it mean to be kind to one's self? What does it mean to accept one's self?

Now we're getting personal, aren't we? Now we're getting a little too close to home. We're hitting some very sensitive areas, I know. We're going into the depths of the self. And in the depths are the shadowy parts that we have difficulty facing and acknowledging are there.

You shall *like* your neighbor as you *like* yourself.
But what if you don't really like yourself very much? What then?

You shall *value* your neighbor as you *value* yourself.
But what if you don't really value yourself very much?

You shall *forgive* your neighbor as you *forgive* yourself.
But what if you can't forgive yourself?

And what about kindness? Do you know how to be kind to yourself? Can you cherish yourself, honor yourself?

Honor, not just part of yourself or even most of yourself, but all of yourself?

You shall *accept* your neighbor as you *accept* yourself.
But can you accept yourself?
Not part of yourself.
Not just your put-together-Sunday-self, not just the part you want people to see, but *all* of yourself. *All*. Can you?

We are made up of many parts. There are parts that see the light of day and parts we place in shadow and lock away from the world and even ourselves. They might be out of sight, but they're never, ever out of mind. They're all there. It's the parts that we lock away or try to forget, that we don't want others to see, or can't acknowledge to ourselves, that we generally have difficulty liking or valuing or honoring or cherishing. We all have parts of ourselves that we struggle to like or accept; there are parts we even despise and hate.

Years ago I came across this very wise saying that I use a lot: "Be kind, for everyone is fighting a hard battle." You never know what someone is struggling with. Very often the ones who seem to have it all together, who appear "perfect," the ones obsessed with perfection and who expect perfection from others, are often the ones who are hurting the most inside, but they can't accept that because that would mean admitting imperfection. We are divided within, and we know it.

The psalms are remarkable in their ability to speak to the human condition. They're written from the heart. When people ask me what they should do when they have difficulty praying, when they can't find the words to pray, I often suggest that they pray the psalms, allow the psalms to give voice to their hearts. It's all there, every aspect of the human condition. The psalmist understands what it means to live with a divided soul, to be at odds with one's self, alienated from God, neighbor. You can hear it particularly in Psalm 86:11, in this petition: "...give me an undivided heart to revere your name." It's a plea from one who knows what it's like to live divided.

Yet the psalmist seeks something more. He wants wholeheartedness. For he knows that wholeheartedness helps us to praise and glorify God. When we're wholehearted—undivided—we're better situated to perceive God's love moving toward us, and when we know this we're free to praise. You see, when we're divided there's always a part of us—the unacceptable, the sinful or shameful part—that doesn't feel worthy of God's love. This, then, only reinforces the division. This is like living in Sheol. Sheol is not necessarily hell but a place where we're cut off from God, with no personality, no strength, no life, living in shades, in shadow.

The psalmist, however, wants to worship God with his whole heart. When the psalmist, undivided, is open to God's love, *then* the soul knows that God is gracious. A divided self has difficulty believing, has difficulty trusting, never really experiences the grace, the steadfast love of God, because that self is harboring a feeling that there is a part that is unlovable, unacceptable, unforgivable. That's the part we have difficulty accepting. That's what we focus on. That's the only part we think God sees.

However, over and over again the psalmist affirms, indeed the Bible insists, that *God is gracious and merciful.* "For great is your steadfast love toward me; you have delivered my soul from the depths of Sheol" (Ps. 86:13). Yet so many can never really "hear" such good news, have never really experienced this grace.

The gospel is this: *God's favor toward us is real, now.* We *already* have God's favor. We *already* dwell in God's favor. We don't have to earn it. We don't have to work toward it. Yet there's something broken or distorted in the human psyche that can't quite accept or believe it, remains suspicious of it. In one of Paul Tillich's (1886-1965) greatest sermons, "You Are Accepted," he has this piercing insight into the experience of grace. Grace can and does strike us. In the midst of our pain, self-alienation, disgust, and self-hatred, in our inability to embrace all of ourselves as God does, a wave of light breaks into our darkness and we begin to hear a voice deep within, deeper than the fearful, negative, critical voice of our egos, a voice of the Holy Spirit that whispers to the depths of our soul: "You are accepted. *You are* accepted, accepted by that which is greater than you.... *Simply accept the fact that you are accepted!*" Tillich writes, "If that happens to us, we experience grace. After such an experience we may not be better than before, and we may not believe more than before. But everything is transformed. In that moment, grace conquers sin, and reconciliation bridges the gulf of estrangement. And nothing is demanded of this experience, no religious or moral or intellectual presupposition, nothing but *acceptance*."[7] Accept your acceptance.

The capacity to love yourself—to like, to forgive, to accept yourself—is not selfish, and it's not a sin. In fact, to love yourself is critical if you're really going to love neighbor, and the stranger, and even God. The ability to love neighbor and stranger flows through our capacity to love and accept ourselves, and the capacity to love ourselves is rooted in God's love for *every* part of ourselves. What's needed is a relationship that mirrors God's own relationship with us, which is rooted and grounded in love. To see ourselves the way God sees us. This is what was driving the apostle Paul and his ministry and why he was willing to suffer loss and persecution, because of this truth: "Owe no one anything, except to love one another; for the one who loves another has fulfilled the law" (Romans 13:8). Indeed, the law is summed up in this word, "Love your neighbor as yourself. Love does no wrong to a neighbor; therefore, love is the fulfilling of the law" (Romans 13:10).

Before we start trying to love our neighbor, we need to start with the one we're with, within. Not in a self-centered, egotistical, narcissistic way, but in a loving way look inward. *If we're looking inward in a truly loving way, we will quite naturally begin to look outward in a loving way. If we're not being loving toward ourselves, then don't be surprised if we have difficulty loving others.*

This is a real concern within the Christian experience today. We think of love as only self-giving love, sacrificial, which sets self aside, sets personal concerns aside, concern only for others. There are a lot of Christians out there doing all kinds of good and necessary things—but their inner lives are wasting away; they're empty and hollow. It's surface Christianity. They're so outward focused they're not attentive to what's occurring in their hearts. As a result, there are a lot of tormented Christian souls around who can't hear the gospel and therefore can't really share it. Or they're so bent on making

---

[7] Paul Tillich, "You Are Accepted," *The Shaking of the Foundations* (New York: Charles Scribner's Sons, 1948), 162. The full text of the sermon may be found here: http://www.religion-online.org/showchapter.asp?title=378&C=84.

everyone think they're Christian or doing the Christian "thing" in service, that they've never applied Christian love to themselves, extended kindness to themselves, acceptance to themselves. I think this one of the reasons why churches can be so dysfunctional and cruel, and why Christians develop a reputation for being a critical, judgmental, nasty group of people. We do to our neighbors what we do to ourselves. We need help loving ourselves.

What do we do? How do we accept ourselves? Accept God's acceptance? It's through grace, of course. The Swiss psychiatrist Carl Jung claimed that, "The most terrifying thing is to accept oneself completely." He's right. We don't want to hear this, but he's right. That's why grace is required. This is difficult. We can't do this alone. We need help, we need grace. I believe self-acceptance and love to be among the critical issues facing us today; it is one of the most pressing ethical issues facing us as Christians. If you want to know what burdens my heart as a pastor, it's this.

Writing toward the end of his life, Jung argued that the "acceptance of oneself is the essence of the whole moral problem and the epitome of a whole outlook on life."[8] Then he addressed his concerns directly at the Church, targeting Christians who pride themselves on their virtuous life and good deeds, yet don't know how to love themselves. The Church needs to hear this today; Christians need to wrestle with what he said because I think Jung gets right to the core of what's wrong within Christianity and what's wrong with so much of the Church these days— *we have yet to fully embrace and embody the implications of the gospel.*[9]

Jung wrote:

> That I feed the hungry, that I forgive an insult, that I love my enemy in the name of Christ—all these are undoubtedly great virtues. What I do unto the least of my brethren, that I do unto Christ. But what if I should discover that the least among them all, the poorest of all the beggars, the most impudent of all the offenders, the very enemy himself—that these are within me, and *that I myself stand in need of the alms of my own kindness— that I myself am the enemy who must be loved*—what then?[10]

What then?

---

[8] Carl G. Jung, "Psychotherapists or the Clergy," *Psychology and Religion, The Collected Works of C. G. Jung,* Vol. 2 (Princeton, NJ: Princeton University Press, 1958), §500.
[9] Carl G. Jung makes this point in "Introduction to the Religious and Psychological Problems of Alchemy," *Psychology and Alchemy, The Collected Works of C. G. Jung,* Vol. 12 (Princeton: Princeton University Press, 1977), §7.
[10] Jung "Psychotherapists or the Clergy." *Emphasis added.*

This work, this inner-work, isn't easy. But we have a moral obligation to ourselves and to the world—to God—to begin it, to continue it, to deepen that capacity to love ourselves. That's what grace does; that's what grace is. We have to start claiming our self-worth, because by grace we are *already* worthy. And so *for the love of God*, please stop raging against yourself and tearing yourself apart, if you're doing this. Stop. Be kind to yourself. Be compassionate toward yourself. Make peace with yourself. What we do to this "neighbor" within, we extend and project out upon the world.

I'll close by offering a gift, a poem by Dereck Walcott (b. 1930), "Love After Love." I had this taped on my bathroom mirror at home for a time. You can hear the Eucharistic aspect of what he's getting at here. To give yourself back to yourself, to be wholehearted, is a holy, sacramental act that we bestow upon ourselves and through us to the world.

> The day will come
> the time will come
> when with elation
>
> you will greet yourself
> arriving at your own door
> and each will smile at each other's welcome
>
> saying sit here, eat
> you will love again the stranger who was yourself
> Give wine, give bread
> give back your heart to yourself
>
> to the stranger who has loved you all your life
> who you ignored for another
> who knows you by heart
>
> Take down the love letters from the bookshelf,
> the photographs, the desperate notes
> feel your own image in the mirror, see it
> Feast on your life.

To give yourself back to yourself, to be wholehearted is a holy, sacramental act that we bestow upon ourselves and through us to the world. Then we can really give ourselves to the world and to God when we truly love ourselves.

Presbyterians & Predestination

Psalm 24 & Ephesians 1:3-14

People can say what they will about John Calvin (1509-1564). And they do. But as Peter Steinfels wrote several years ago in *The New York Times*, marking the 500th anniversary of his birth—Friday was Calvin's birthday, he would be 506 today—Calvin was "a religious thinker and leader who may have done as much as anyone to shape the modern world."[1] Calvin's often associated with the doctrine of predestination, and then he's quickly dismissed because we assume we know what he meant by the word. People often confuse predestination with predeterminism (or just determinism)—but they are not the same. Calvin did not advocate for predeterminism. He was an advocate of predestination or, simply, what theologians call the doctrine of election.

As one of the theological heirs of Calvin, Presbyterians are often associated with the doctrine of predestination; it's sometimes all that people know about us. I've been in many conversations that go something like this: "You're a Presbyterian? How do you spell that? Oh, you're the ones that believe in predestination." And then they ask, "Do you really believe that?" And then I say that I do.

Around the edge of two pages at the center of *The Presbyterian Handbook*, a whimsical yet informative overview of Presbyterianism, with an illustration of Cool Calvin wearing sunglasses, you'll find a black border that reads: WARNING: IT MAY TAKE MULTIPLE READINGS—AND TIME—TO UNDERSTAND THIS CONCEPT.[2] The concept? Predestination. Let's look at what it is—and isn't. Let's go back to Calvin.

The contemporary novelist Marilynne Robinson, author of the Pulitzer-prize winning *Gilead* (one of my favorite novels), is a huge fan of Calvin. She's a deacon in her church in Iowa and has been reading Calvin for years—for fun! She also reads Calvin in order to make her life better, and therefore commends him to the church. She claims that reading Calvin's beautiful French prose has made her a better writer, but more than anything, in reading Calvin (his sermons, his commentaries on scripture, his masterful *Institutes*), she has come to see the glory and wonder and amazement of God pouring through his writings. When Calvin wrote about theology, about God, he was

---

[1] Peter Steinfels, *The New York Times*, July 4, 2009.
http://www.nytimes.com/2009/07/04/us/04beliefs.html.
[2] *The Presbyterian Handbook* (Louisville: Geneva Press, 2006).

not interested in rational speculative considerations of the divine, which, as he put it, "Flits about in the brain doing nothing."[3]

The doctrine that consumed Calvin, and you can see it in the first ten pages of the *Institutes*, was the doctrine of creation. What I mean by this is not creationism, although Calvin believed in a literal reading of Genesis, but a view of the glory of God found in the created order, which, to the eyes of faith, gives profound witness to the love of God in Jesus Christ. Calvin said, "There is not one blade of grass, there is no color in this world that is not intended to make us rejoice," and, therefore, we are "not only to be spectators in this beautiful theatre but to enjoy the vast bounty and variety of good things which are displayed to us in it."[4]

Calvin approached this amazing world, the "theatre of God's glory," as he liked to say, with awe, amazement, or as he said, "wonderment." God's rule over the creation is sovereign. Our lives are held in the sovereignty of God. The beauty of creation overwhelmed Calvin, as did the beauty of God (yes, *beauty*), the God who has called, claimed, loved, and redeemed us in Jesus Christ. And so Calvin invites us to serve this God in the theatre of God's glory, the world. Robinson reminds us that "Calvin was a product of Renaissance humanism, a student of Greek and Roman classics who reread Cicero [106 BC-43 BC] every year, a writer of exceptional grace and lucidity in both Latin and French, a man of prodigious learning, who did not dwell on damnation but rather exulted in a sovereign but not at all distant God, a God whose glory was manifest in the goodness of the world and the potential of humanity."[5]

Calvin believed the entire creation is shouting out the glory of God, shouting out the love of God, shouting out the redemptive power of God's concern for us, all the time. Some see it, others don't. And the reason people can't see it—that is, naturally, unaided—is because of the power of sin. Due to sin we can't see what's clearly there in front of our eyes. Because of selfishness or egocentricity, because of our brokenness, of our refusal to live into the vision God has for us in Christ, we turn our eyes, and so we fall. We have to stop thinking of the Fall in Genesis as something that occurred once a long time ago. Every time we turn our face away from God, we fall. Every time we turn away, we fall—again and again and again.

---

[3] John Calvin, cited in a lecture by Serene Jones, "Calvin, Creation, and the Holy Spirit." Calvin Jubilee, Montreat, NC, July 9, 2009.
[4] From Calvin's Commentary on Psalm 104:331, quoted by William J. Bouwsma, *John Calvin: A Sixteenth Century Portrait* (New York: Oxford University Press, 1988), 135.
[5] Steinfels.

This is the human condition. Calvin called it "total depravity." This is *not* to say that there is no good in us, because there is; it *is* to say that there's no area of our lives that is so pure, so perfect, so good, so loving that we can freely choose the pure, the perfect, the good; there's no place in our lives unaffected by the brokenness, the woundedness of the human condition. It's total. It's comprehensive. Sin is a problem—a huge problem. It constantly interferes with our ability to enjoy God—and we're supposed to enjoy God. But we can't will our way out of this predicament by being good.

Remember the story of "The Little Engine That Could," who made it to the top of the mountain through an effort of thought and will? "I think I can. I think I can." From a biblical perspective this is a deceptive strategy when it comes to God, or following Christ. I recently discovered that an early version of this story first appeared in the *New York Tribune*, April 8, 1906, as part of a sermon by the Rev. Charles S. Wing. A brief version of the tale appeared under the title *Thinking One Can* in 1906, in *Wellspring for Young People*, a Sunday School publication. It's a fun story, but it's lousy theology. Theologically speaking, we have to "throw out the engine that could because you can't."[6]

We can't work our way toward God. We are flawed through and through, every one of us, if not all the time, then often. We are continually dependent upon on the graciousness of God to intervene, to do for us what we can never do for ourselves—namely, to freely choose God and love God completely with all our mind, soul, heart, and strength (Luke 10:27). Theologian Paul Lehmann (1906-1994) once said that Calvin's doctrine of total depravity was a "most hopeful of all doctrines."[7] That might sound odd. Why hopeful? Because it acknowledges that the source of our salvation and the course of our eternal destiny are not contingent upon our ability to choose or believe or be good or be perfect, or whatever.

Think about it. To believe the source of my salvation is dependent upon something that I have to do, some good work or collection of works I have to do to make God happy—to believe that salvation is contingent upon something I have earned, the result of having proved myself worthy of God's love and acceptance—to believe that God's acceptance of me is dependent upon my ability to completely believe and trust one hundred percent in God—this would the worst possible sentence inflicted upon me. That's not good news, gospel. In fact, it would be terrible news. That would be hell. Because then I would be left in an awful state: knowing my own brokenness and my woundedness and the tragic flaws in my own life. I would never be

---

[6] Cynthia L. Rigby in her lecture, "Calvin and the Wondrous Glory of God." Calvin Jubilee, Montreat, NC, July 8, 2009. I'm indebted to Cindy's lecture for providing a larger theological context in which to frame the doctrine of election.
[7] Cited by Rigby.

able to live up to some idealized vision of what I think God wants from me. That would not be grace, but something else; it would be the opposite of grace.

Grace is God's eternal, free choice to say *Yes* to me through Jesus Christ. Grace is God's *Yes* to you through Jesus Christ. Because salvation is a gift that cannot be earned, it has to be given, offered—and it has already been given through the grace of God revealed in life of Jesus Christ. God elects us, God chooses us, God makes the first move toward us. Calvin had such a high view of election—of predestination—not because he created the idea (he didn't), but because it's found all over scripture. God elects Abraham and his children and calls them to be a blessing to the world. Abram didn't wake up one day and say to himself "Let's say we leave home in Haran with the family, go to a distant, unknown territory, and begin to follow a new, alien God." God chooses people to be kings and priests and prophets. Jesus calls the disciples; they did not choose him first. Even Jesus Christ is the elect of God through whom God chooses to redeem the world. The idea of election emerges in Paul's letter, especially this one to the Ephesians.

Through his experience of Jesus Christ, Paul came to understand—not in an intellectual way, but in an existential, heart-felt way—that he was accepted in God's sight, not through any works of the law or merits, but through the glorious grace revealed in Jesus Christ. These verses, 3-14, make up one long sentence in Greek; it's an effusive, dynamic, (over)flowing expression of affirmation that leads to a crescendo of confession. Calvin says, "Christ ... is the mirror, in which it behooves us to contemplate our election; and here we may do it with safety."[8] Jesus Christ has set us free, and this freedom is granted to those who are far off from God and those who are near. We are abundantly free—accepted completely, through and through, in the eyes of God. For it is God's plan, revealed in Jesus, to bring *all* people together into one people. God is working God's purpose out through everyone and everything. Jesus takes us up into the high places with him, with God, to find communion with God. Jesus takes us, escorts us into the presence of God—because we would never be able to get there on our own. Election is God's plan to include us in the work of salvation through Jesus Christ. Didn't Jesus say, "You did not choose, but I chose you" (John 15:16)?

Now all of this might come as quite a shock to our egos. Our egos operate with the assumption that we're in control of our lives. The ego thinks that it's all about itself all the time. This doctrine is a jolt to our system because we like to believe that we can choose what we believe and what we don't

---

[8] John Calvin, *Institutes of the Christian Religion* (1559), III.xxiv.5

believe, that we control our destinies, that we're responsible for our own salvation. The bad news to the ego is this: *No, you're not.*

But we know that there's more to us than our egos. *No, you're not in control* is regarded by the depths of our souls as good news. The soul rejoices in knowing that God is God. And, therefore, God always makes the first move toward us. Even when we think we made the first move, it was God placing this yearning within us, illuminating the deepest desires of our hearts. In our faith and in our doubt, searching after God, God is always drawing us into relationship with God.

The eminent twentieth century Swiss theologian Karl Barth (1886-1968) was a theological heir of Calvin. He stressed, through a reading of Ephesians 1:3-14, that when God said *Yes* to Jesus in raising him from the grave, when God said *Yes* to Jesus:

> God has reached out to say Yes to all human beings in Jesus Christ. This singular and potent *Yes* is the true biblical doctrine of election. It is not that God is bound to some and unbound to others. In the biblical doctrine of predestination, God is bound to each one of us by being bound to Jesus Christ in his life, death, and resurrection.[9]

Barth's statement on predestination attempts to clear up some of the misappropriations of Calvin. The Calvinists came along after Calvin and wanted to determine who was among the elect and who wasn't. The doctrine of election should not be used in this way. Barth's reading of the doctrine leans in the direction of saying that God's *Yes* in Christ includes all of humanity and that we're all saved. Who is in? Who is out? That's not for us to decide. Grace and with it election, for the two are related, "teaches that each of our lives is rooted in the gracious will and intentionality of God." It's meant to be a doctrine of encouragement and hope.[10]

Why? Because God is working through us and is committed to us and will never leave us or abandon us. Why? Because God has work for us to do. Election is never a condition of privilege, but responsibility. Abraham and through him Israel were called, chosen, not because they were better, but because God had a job for them to do—to be a blessing to the world.

When we meditate on and contemplate God's grace toward us, the reality of our election—that God has actually chosen us—we soon discover that God

---

[9] Cited by William Stacy Johnson, *John Calvin: Reformer for the 21st Century* (Louisville: Westminster John Knox Press, 2009), 48.
[10] Johnson, 42.

has something in store for us, a new way to live and love, a new job to do, a new task, a project, a witness, a ministry—something.

This grace, this glorious grace is an extraordinary gift. To be chosen, to be elected, to be included in God's redemptive plan and purpose is an amazing gift. As Paul suggests in this text, we're grafted, "adopted," into God's plan—because God has work for us to do. When we remember our election, we find ourselves empowered to serve, to live, to love in new ways—to enjoy God in new ways.

God might have elected us from the foundations of the world, but the working out of that salvation is not yet complete. We work out our salvation individually, but also in and through the community—it's what the church is for. We might be elected, chosen by God in grace, but God isn't finished with us yet, no matter our age.

The poet Maya Angelou (1928-2014) expressed her amazement at people who boast that they are saved, who think that their growth in grace stops with their profession of faith, or who are confident in their status as Christians. "You are a Christian?" she asks of them, of us. And she adds, "Already?"[11]

The Christian life for Paul, for Calvin, for us as a people reformed and always being reformed, is *living into* the people we are by God's glorious grace through Jesus Christ and sealed by the Holy Spirit forever in the depths of our hearts. We are called to *live into* our election. *Thanks be to God.*

---

[11] Cited in Johnson, 45.

Caring with a Shepherd's Heart

Psalm 23, John 10:11-18 & 1 John 3:18-24

The image of the shepherd is near and dear to the hearts of both Jews and Christians. There is no better-known psalm than the twenty-third, most likely written by David, the shepherd who became king, the *shepherd-king*. Many have this psalm memorized—and for some only the King James Version will do. This psalm with all its majesty and beauty dwells deep within our heart of hearts; it's tucked away deep within us. It's a part of us. It provides extraordinary comfort and assurance and hope. It is often read or understood as a petition or plea or a prayer used in difficult situations, used to summon up enough faith in order to believe that Yahweh is indeed my shepherd.[1]

But this is more than just a petition or plea. Hebrew poetry, like Celtic poetry, is making a statement, making a strong non-refutable claim about reality and God. This psalm is a confession, a statement, an affirmation. It's not "Lord will you please be my shepherd." The psalmist is a staking a claim on the divine presence. Yahweh—you are my Shepherd. Right now. This shepherd metaphor "evokes a wise, caring, attentive agent who watches over, feeds, and protects a flock that is vulnerable, exposed, dependent, and in need of help," not unlike the work of a mother.[2]

Yahweh, you are my shepherd. Right now. Therefore, I lack nothing. The psalmist is not pointing to sometime in the future when Yahweh will take care of him and provide for his every need. The psalmist is saying at this very moment, here and now, Yahweh, You are my shepherd. You care for my every need; therefore, I lack nothing. And because you are watching out for me, I can relax. I can sit beside the still waters. Because I know you are watching out for me, Yahweh, the stress and worry and concern that I carry around when I forget that You're looking out for me are now gone and my soul has been restored—my soul is healed because I know that I don't have to fend for myself. And this is good news. Even when I am in the pit of hell and everything seems to be crumbling all around me, I fear no evil. For you are my shepherd—and nothing can harm me. And because you are my shepherd—now and always—there will never come a time when You aren't watching out for me, caring for me, Yahweh. Whether now or in the life to

---

[1] On Yahweh as shepherd in the Hebrew tradition see Walter Brueggemann, *Theology of the New Testament: Testimony, Dispute, Advocacy* (Minneapolis, MN: Fortress Press, 1997), 259.
[2] See Brueggemann, 259.

come, I am yours and you are mine. And nothing is going to change this—nothing, not sin, not evil, not even death itself. Nothing.

The image of Yahweh as shepherd takes on flesh in Jesus who said, "I am the good shepherd." He is more than a metaphor. He is the real thing. This is a very significant statement. Unfortunately, too often Jesus' claim has been domesticated and made into something as docile as a well-behaved sheep. "Good" has been equated with "nice." It's sometimes (mis)understood as, "I am the nice shepherd." But "good" doesn't do justice to the text. It's not that Jesus is a well-behaved shepherd who really knows how to do his job without offending anyone. The Greek word for "good" is *agathos*. In this text, John reads, *kalos*. *Kalos* means "noble." Jesus is really saying, "I am the noble shepherd." By "noble" Jesus is claiming for himself an identity and authority reserved for Yahweh. "Noble" refers to Jesus' kingly rule over every other political and social authority.

Jesus is being very intentional here. He is placing himself in that long line of shepherd-kings that began with David, who led his people with compassion and with power, with justice and with love. The Old Testament prophets promised that another shepherd-king would come, like David, who would lead the people with equity, justice, and peace. The shepherd is a metaphor of governance.[3] By describing himself as the noble shepherd, Jesus is claiming for himself the very same symbol and image of Yahweh found through the Old Testament.

And not only is Jesus claiming this image for himself; he's taking upon himself the divine name. Remember when Moses encountered the burning bush on the mountain and the voice summoned him to go to Egypt to liberate the Israelites? Moses said, "Who are you? I don't even know your name." That's when the voice revealed its name. What did the voice say? Tell Pharaoh, "I AM" sent you. I AM is technically the true name of the Living One of Israel, otherwise known as God. In Hebrew it is *'eyeh 'asher 'eyeh* and can be translated, "I was who was. I am who I am. I will be who I will be." (See Exodus 3:13-15) The first letter of each word in the Hebrew is Y-H-W-H (known as the Tetragrammaton)—fill in the vowels and you have Yahweh. Yahweh is the true name of the God of Israel. Yahweh's name actually means I AM.

This means God is a verb—the verb to be. Yahweh is not a static noun or like a modifier, an adverb or adjective, but a verb. From this we learn that God's Being is dynamic, active, and does things.[4] Yahweh has called all things

---

[3] See Brueggemann.

[4] Hiroshi Obayashi, *Agape and History: A Theological Essay on Historical Consciousness* (Washington, DC: University Press of America, 1981), 75ff. The Hebrew verb *hayah* (to be) "is an action

into being, and existence itself is sustained by the abiding presence of God's being. The fact that you are, that you exist, that you can say, "I am," is because you have been called into being by the One who is I AM. To be created in the image of this God is to participate in the Being of God.

And because God's name is holy, it should be unpronounceable. Instead of saying Yahweh, Jews then and now say *Adonai*, which means "Lord." When you see LORD capitalized in the Old Testament, the Hebrew word that stands behind it is actually YHWH. So that when the psalmist says, "The LORD is my shepherd, I shall not want," it's Yahweh, the great I AM being itself who is my shepherd.

And then Jesus goes even further. All those "I am" statements in John ("I am the way, the truth, and the life" (John 14:6). "I am the resurrection and the life" (John 11:25). "I am the bread of life" (John 6:35) gets Jesus into trouble with the authorities because he is claiming the divine name for himself. So not only does Jesus take the shepherd image upon himself, meaning that he will be the true governor of our lives, clearly identifying himself with the God of Israel, but he is claiming that he is divine. He is I AM. So that we come to see that "Jesus is the human repository of all the powers and functions of Israel's LORD."5 "I am the noble shepherd."

As our noble shepherd, Jesus has taken on the responsibility of caring for our lives. And not only our lives, but the life of the world. His life and work set the standard for our life and work. His life and work set the standard for all those who seek to be shepherds in our lives. And his life and work set the standard for those in authority over us, for they have been given a mandate to care for the needs of the people.

The nobility of our Lord is most evident when we see him caring not only for his own sheep but for the wider world. This text thus sets the pattern for the work of his church. The Christian reaches out and lives in the world (without being defined by it), caring for the needs of all people the way a shepherds tends to his flock. In fact, Jesus says we must not only be concerned about our own flock but other flocks, too. Jesus has many flocks and continues to work for that time when there will be one shepherd and one flock.

This text provides a framework for us to reach out to flocks or communities of people who are different or strange or might even make us uncomfortable, even with flocks that don't look like flocks, in order to bring all the separate

---

verb, denoting a decided act of being, becoming and occurring," whereby "being" is inseparable from "becoming."
5 Gerard Sloyan, *John* (Atlanta, GA: John Knox Press, 1988), 128.

flocks into one. Dietrich Bonhoeffer (1906-1945) said the Christian has a moral obligation to care for the weakest and most vulnerable in society, whether they are Christian or not.[6] This is love lived out in truth and action (1 John 3:18). This text speaks to the inclusive nature of the gospel and of our need to bring dissimilar people together in order to find a unity in Christ. This is the goal that Jesus himself sets up for himself—not for us—and therefore it is not debatable. "I have other sheep, that are not of this fold; I must bring them also, and they will heed my voice. So there shall be one flock, one shepherd."

If we are following Jesus, if our wills are aligned with his will, if we are honestly praying, "Thy will be done," then we should be engaged in similar work. We will succeed sometimes and we will fail most of the time, but our job remains the same: do not stand in the way of the shepherd.

But when we fail in our daily living, even when those who care for us fail in their tasks, even when governments relinquish their responsibility to care for society, when we are not in the will of God, when we get in the way—Jesus is still our shepherd. When we recite the 23rd Psalm or read John 10, we are reminded "that Jesus is our only shepherd, the one whose voice [alone] we must heed, and that we must [also] confess that often we listen to the call of wolves and lazy hirelings," people who will always lead us astray. When we recite the 23rd Psalm or read John 10, we ascribe to Jesus prerogatives that the state normally takes on for itself. It is not the state but the shepherd Jesus who is to provide for our health; the shepherd Jesus who ensures our security; the shepherd Jesus who protects us and provides for us."[7] Jesus is watching out for us; he alone restores our souls. We are his and he is ours and nothing can change this fact. "What is your only comfort, in life and in death?" the Heidelberg Catechism (1563) asks us. The answer? "That I belong—body and soul, in life and in death—not to myself but to my faithful Savior, Jesus Christ." This is the Good News! This is the Gospel. Yahweh be praised!

---

[6] "The church is the church only when it exists for others." Dietrich Bonhoeffer, *Letters and Papers from Prison*, edited by Eberhard Bethge (New York: Macmillan Publishing, 1972), 382.
[7] Andrew Warner, "Hooked on War," *The Christian Century* (May 3, 2003), 22.

Seeking After Jesus

Jeremiah 31:31-34 & John 12:20-33

"Sir, we would see Jesus." As I step into the pulpit here to preach each week I see these words. Not in my imagination. I see them literally – they're etched right on the edge of the pulpit. "Sir, we would see Jesus." It's the King James rendering of John 20:21; the New Revised Standard Version says, "Sir, we wish to see Jesus." *Would* or *wish*, both words give expression to their desire—the yearning, the request of these "Greeks" to meet Jesus.

We don't know much about these "Greeks," but we do know something. They're in Jerusalem. They're part of a group of people "who went up," John says, "to worship." By "up" John is referring to the Temple Mount, the temple to Yahweh. They were there to worship for a "festival," referring to Passover. These are people who worshipped Yahweh. But were they Jews? Possibly. They might have been Hellenistic Jews, Jews from the diaspora living in the Greek-speaking world (perhaps from modern Greece or Turkey). Perhaps they were pilgrims, making a once-in-a-lifetime journey to celebrate Passover in Jerusalem. Or they could have been what we might call today religious seekers, Gentiles who worshipped Yahweh but who never became, technically, Jews. They would have been allowed to worship God in the Court of the Gentiles, one of the outer courtyards of the Temple, but not allowed to get much closer than that. Either way, they're religious seekers, there to worship.

That's about all we know. We don't know how they came to know about Jesus. We don't know why they're seeking after him, what draws them toward him. What about Jesus do they find attractive, what draws them to his message and, more than the message, what draws them to him? What we can say is that it's the occasion of worship, informed by a holy curiosity that draws them to him. Their journey toward Jesus traverses through the way of worship, of adoration and praise. It's on the way toward the worship of God that they seek out Philip, "Sir, we wish to see Jesus." Philip went and told Andrew and then Andrew and Philip went and told Jesus. Jesus answered "them," the text says—Philip and Andrew; he never does speak to the Greeks.

And the answer, you have to admit, is a bit odd, starting at verse 23. "The hour has come for the Son of Man to be glorified. Very truly, I tell you, unless a grain of wheat falls into the earth and dies, it remains just a single grain; but if it dies, it bears much fruit. Those who love their life lose it, and those who hate their life in this world will keep it for eternal life. Whoever serves me must follow me, and where I am, there will my servant be also. Whoever serves me, the Father will honor." Talk about *non-sequiturs*! It's a baffling metaphor upon first hearing it. Learning that "some Greeks" seek to see him, Jesus launches into this mini-sermon.

From our vantage we know that Jesus is talking with Philip and Andrew about his impending death and the meaning of the death. Because the implied reference is to the cross, a lot of ink has been spent and spilled over the centuries trying to make sense of these verses—and, for the most part ignoring the *setting* for Jesus' statement, the inquiry of Greeks on their way to worship Yahweh. Commentators tend to reflect on verse 23 and following.

The Church has come up with all kind of theories regarding the meaning of the crucifixion, what theologians call theories of atonement. The most pervasive theory in Western theology, running from Ambrose of Milan (c. between 337 and 340-397) to Anselm of Canterbury (c.1003-1109) right up to Mel of Hollywood, (although I really shouldn't place Mel Gibson in the company of Ambrose and Milan), is that "God demands death in order for life to emerge, that only a violent sacrifice of a perfect and sinless Jesus could appease a God whose honor has been affronted and whose anger has been aroused." This is the prevailing view in the Church; many are not aware that there are other views. So many Christians over the years—including today—and many non-Christians believe that "God is basically an angry Father who demands sacrifice in order to balance the injustice of the universe caused by human sin." Contemporary theologian Michael Welker says this view is "nothing less than destructive of faith." It has "propagated a latent image of God that is deeply unchristian, indeed demonic: This God is always seeking compensation."[1] I would agree with him. This view is so ingrained into the Christian experience that when we hear a text like this, of falling and dying, of a death required, we hear it with sacrifice in mind.

As it stands, this verse is problematic. It's problematic because it's so easy to think that a follower of Jesus must despise this world and that we are to hate our lives within it. Many Christians are running around with this view. This was the view I had as a young adult. I'm not sure where I got it from—my parents didn't hold this view, my church didn't, I can't remember my church school teachers saying this. I read a lot of religious literature when I was in high school, which, upon looking back now, I now know, was really more fundamentalist in nature. This did a lot of damage to my psyche.

In this text, Jesus seems to be saying that life has no inherent value unless it dies. He seems to be warning against loving life. This has led some Christians

---

[1] I'm grateful for Thomas G. Long's succinct summary of substitutionary atonement theory and for the Welker quotation, "What God Wants," *The Christian Century* (March 21, 2006), 19.

to assume that loving the world too much, having fun, taking pleasure in the world and enjoying the beauty of people and creation is a sin, a threat, a temptation that needs to be confessed and repented from.

Jesus' statements here also appear to be otherworldly. This, too, has led some Christians to believe that this world means nothing, only the after-life matters. These are generally the same folks who argue that we don't have to be stewards of creation, don't have to be concerned about climate change, or social injustice, or even the threat of nuclear annihilation because this world doesn't matter.

Some Christians believe that Jesus' ministry and message have little to do with this world; it's really more about our eternal destiny, where we go when we die. This view runs deep in our theological DNA; that Jesus had to die on the cross in order for us to go to heaven. John Chrysostom (c.347-407) wrote, "Since, if anyone look to heaven and see the beauteous things there, he will soon despise this life, and make no account of it."[2] For him, God's Kingdom is the afterlife. To focus on this life is, as he put it, "a kind of chain." One of my professors at Princeton, Diogenes Allen, reminded us that the Christian life is about more than *geography*—worrying about whether one goes "up" or "down" after one dies. It's easy to believe that this is what Jesus was concerned about because he refers to "eternal life," which we assume (incorrectly) here that Jesus is referring to the afterlife – which is most clearly not the case.

And there are other questions. What does it really mean to hate one's life? What does it mean to die to self? How does one lose one's soul? This is a tough one. Here, too, a misreading of this text has done considerable damage. If one's soul or self (the Greek here is *psyche*) is lost, then what is left? Does Christ become everything and we becoming nothing? Is this what it means to be a Christian, losing our individuality, our uniqueness? I've met a lot of Christians who said they are trying to become nothing so that Christ can become everything in them. It's as if they're describing a kind of spirit-possession. This isn't healthy. Imagine how an interpretation like this sounds to someone who's been emotionally or physically abused, who has a poor sense of self, who was taught that they don't matter, the trauma of their experience belittled, their trust betrayed, their soul broken and diminished; and what about women and men who have had to struggle throughout their lives to find their souls, to regain and reclaim their souls, who have learned to care for their souls, to love themselves, honor themselves, respect

---

[2] John Chrysostom, *Homilies on the Gospel of St. John and Epistle to the Hebrews*, LXVVI, http://www.ccel.org/ccelschaff/npnf114.iv.lxix.html.

themselves? Hearing Jesus say they must "hate their life" is not good news! In fact, it's really bad news, terrible news.

Surely Jesus knows all of this. I can't imagine that Jesus, teaching in love, would have meant us to read or hear the text this way! There has to be a still more excellent way.

Psychologist Mary Tennes suggests that it's important for us to differentiate between *submission* and *surrender*.

Submission means giving over what is true and authentic about ourselves, giving it up because another demands it—even though it may crush your spirit. When we submit, we do so out of fear that the person who demands our submission will hurt us or abandon us if we refuse. Submission always means diminishment of the self. It's the opposite of abundant life."[3]

It's worth highlighting this reference to abundant life here because *abundant life* is actually a better way of translating "eternal life"—or life touched by eternity. It means overflowing life, "life that spills over the edges like a sloshing water bucket."[4] It's eternal in the sense that it has no limit, it's unending, and therefore God's life is abundant, vital, creative, full to overflowing.

Surrender, on the other hand, is not giving ourselves over to another out of fear, but rather, giving ourselves over to a larger vision of what we are most deeply meant to be and do in God's world. Much of what we cling to and strive for in our daily lives comes from a restricted range of possibility.

Submission is motivated by fear, but surrender is motived by hope, she suggests.[5] Tennes is very helpful here. Surrender calls us to risk, to give up the familiar, to strike out for unknown territory. Isn't this what Jesus did on the cross?

What Jesus is getting at here in this text is really about surrender, not submission. The ability to surrender is motivated by hope; we might also call it faith. I would modify this slightly and suggest that there's something deeper that motivates surrender within us. *Surrender is motivated by love.*

---

[3] Pamela Cooper-White's summary of Mary Tennes' article, "Beyond Submission and Toward Surrender: The Evolving Female Self," unpublished paper, cited in Cooper-White, *The Cry of Tamar: Violence Against Women and the Church's Response* (Minneapolis: Fortress Press, 1995), 93.
[4] Mary H. Schertz, Exegesis notes for the Fifth Sunday in Lent, *Lectionary Homiletics*, XXIII (No. 2, February/March 2012), 57.
[5] Cooper-White on Tennes, Pastoral implications for the Fifth Sunday in Lent, *Lectionary Homiletics*, XXIII (No. 2, February/March 2012), 59.

This is why I think it's critical for us to hear these verses about dying and rising within the larger setting of the text that begins with "some Greeks" making their way into worship with a desire, a passion, a love for God. It is the context of love that these Greeks desire to *see Jesus*. If my reading of this is correct, we then discover that there is a kind of knowledge of God, a type of insight, awareness, perception of God that can *only* be found by following after the desires of our hearts and adoration—doxology. I'm talking about a knowledge of God that can't be achieved or accessed by our intellect or by living a good life. What if there are things about God that we discover only in and through worship rooted and grounded in love and not apart form it?[6]

I believe that it's the context of love—drawn by the love of God, called by the love of God, claimed and affirmed to the core of our being by the power of God's love—that allows us to see Jesus, to see the God who shines through face of Jesus. And within love we can hear in this text something profound. A deep and mysterious wisdom is found here, friends, a wisdom that takes us a very long time to fathom: *in order for a life to truly glorify God, to fulfill its purpose, something within us has to die. Something has to die.* We don't want to hear this. But the part of us that doesn't want to hear this is not the true self, but the *ego* or the *false self*.

It seems to me that this is what Jesus is talking about here. It's our human egocentricity that needs to die, to be knocked off dead-center (and I mean this literally), so that Christ can become the center. It's the false self (which is often fear-based) that needs to die so that the true self, feeling loved, grounded in its identity in Christ, may emerge. And this can't occur without some kind of assault on our sensibilities and reason (like the crucifixion itself), without something that destabilizes the ego, a force that throws us into conflict, what I would call a kind of *gracious violence*—with an emphasis on gracious.[7] Either way, Jesus' call to die can only be "heard" or received or accepted by the ego or the false self within the wider framework of God's love—when fear is replaced with love—when we come to acknowledge that God does not ultimately seek to destroy life, but to give life, abundantly. Jesus said, I have come that they might have life and have it in abundance (John 10:10). We come to know this truth and welcome it—dying and rising and bearing fruit—within a trusting relationship, within the context of worship

---

[6] Kenneth E. Kovacs, Theological themes for the Fifth Sunday in Lent, *Lectionary Homiletics*, XXIII (No. 2, February/March 2012), 58.
[7] Kovacs, 58. This notion of "gracious violence" is heavily informed by the novelist Flannery O'Connor (1925-1964), especially her short story "Revelation;" as well as the convictional theology of James E. Loder (1931-2001) and C. G. Jung's understanding of ego-transformation. There is no transformation without conflict.

of a God who came "not to condemn the world, but that the world might be saved" (John 3:17).

The ego or false self within us—often full of fear—hears these words of Jesus as submission. The true self, on the other hand, – grounded in love—hears Jesus' words as surrender, a *joyous surrender*, as an opportunity to embrace one's destiny and purpose.

Last year I came across these words of the poet Kathleen Raine (1909-2003), so simple, yet so profound: "Unless you see a thing in the light of love, you do not see a thing at all."[8] It's worth praying and meditating on this for a long time. Implicit here, of course, is the opposite; without the light of love, we don't see a thing, including Jesus.

To see Jesus—*and to see who he really is*—requires a change within us. Something has to die within us; something has to shift; something has to give way. The change, the shift, doesn't occur through fear, only *love*. There's not much gained in this world through living a life of fear. Fear doesn't motivate this change, love does. It's finally love that motivates us to surrender. We are not asked to submit, but we are called to *surrender*—and we can—

because the one who calls us *is* love,
and the one to whom we yield *is* love,
and the one into whom we fall
and fall
and fall
and discover abundant life *is* love.

---

[8] I'm grateful to Melanie Starr Costello for introducing me to Raine's poetry. This quote is cited in John O'Donohue's (1956-2008), *Anam Cara: A Book of Celtic Wisdom* (HarperCollins, 1989), 65.

Life in the Spirit

Romans 8:1-11

Here's a story about a dog. Martin Laird teaches in the theology and religious studies department at Villanova University. In his book, *Into the Silent Land: A Guide to the Christian Practice of Contemplation*, he recounts an encounter he once had walking along open fields (probably in England). He would take this route whenever he needed to clear his head. He often saw a man walking his four Kerry blue terriers. "These were amazing dogs," he relates. "Bounding energy, elastic grace, and electric speed, they coursed and leapt through open fields. It was invigorating just to watch these muscular stretches of freedom race along." Three of the four dogs acted this way. The fourth stayed behind and, off to the side of its owner, ran in tight circles. Laird never understood why he did this; the dog had all the room in the world to leap and bound. One day he asked the owner, "Why does your dog do that? Why does it run in little circles instead of running with the others?" He explained that "before he acquired the dog, it had lived practically all its life in a cage and could only exercise by running in circles. To run meant running in tight circles."[1]

Laird writes that this event has stayed with him as a "powerful metaphor of the human condition." This is how Laird puts it: "For indeed we are free, as the Psalmist insists, 'My heart like a bird has escaped from the snare of the fowler'" (Ps. 123:7). But the memory of the cage remains. And so we run in tight, little circles, even while immersed in open fields of grace and freedom."[2]

Although Laird cites Psalm 123, last week I said he could have just as easily quoted from Galatians 5, or from here in Romans 8:1 and 2: "There is therefore now no condemnation for those who are in Christ Jesus. For the law of the Spirit of life in Christ Jesus has set you free from the law of sin and of death." Paul offers these words, indeed this entire chapter, as part of his concluding remarks regarding the Jewish law, the nature of sin, justification, and the new life we have in Christ. Paul is treading through deep theological waters in these chapters, addressing issues and concerns that, in many ways, are not as central to our lives today. But Paul has something to say to us, the Spirit still has something to say to us. In order for this text to

---

[1] Martin Laird, *Into the Silent Land: A Guide to the Christian Practice of Contemplation* (New York: Oxford University Press, 2010), 19-20.
[2] Laird, 20.

speak to us today, we, too, must be willing to tread some deep theological waters. So let's go deep.

Paul is writing to Jewish and Gentile Christians in Rome who struggle over whether one has to first become an ethical Jew by following Torah, the Law, before becoming a follower of Christ. For Jews following Jesus it's a question of whether or not Torah, the Law (the 610 laws of the Mosaic covenant), needs to be followed or not. The Law was viewed as the way toward righteousness, that is, toward a right relationship with God. Follow the Law and all will be well.

But through his experience in Christ, Paul came to know of another "law," a deeper force, a dynamic, contravening tendency at work in the lives of everyone who attempts to live according to Torah: the power of sin. Note that I said "sin" in the singular, not "sins." In Paul's theological worldview, sin is not so much an *act* as much as it is a *force*; that is, a power at work outside us in the world and also within us. Due to the influence of this force—a power that is at odds with God's will, a power at work in the world and in us that seeks to tear us away from God—a power that's hostile to God, that seduces us into believing that we matter more than God, that we can live apart from God, that we can make choices as if God doesn't exist, a kind of egotism that puts us at the center of our universe. Due to this power, human beings are bound, enslaved, trapped, caught, and foiled in their attempt to follow God's will, the law. This is how Paul understands sin. Because of the influence of this power, we sin and commit sins.

"Sin" is also synonymous with another word in Paul's vocabulary—which has caused all kinds of confusion across the years—flesh. "Flesh," *sarx* in Greek, is Paul's word for humanity that is under the influence of the power of sin. Flesh does not mean "body;" Paul is not saying the body is sinful; to suggest so is a misreading. Suggesting that the body is the cause of sin has led to all kinds of distorted views of sexuality within the Christian experience that continue to wreak havoc upon the church. The body is not sinful, not any more than any other part of ourselves, bound as we are by the force of sin. If Paul meant our physical bodies, he would have used the word "soma."

There's also another word he uses in a way similar to *sin* and *flesh*, as a kind of force, it is death. Death, too, is a kind of force that is at odds with life. It's a force that tears down, breaks down, destroys—life, lives, souls, relationships, justice, hope—and works against God's desire for life and soul and relationships, justice and hope. This is Paul's view of the human condition.

Paul knows there's something in this world that holds us captive, that hinders and hampers our ability to love, to forgive, to be generous, to be agents of justice—to do God's will. If we're honest with ourselves and analyze our feelings and experience, we know he's right. Sometimes it feels like there's a force outside us, that we are the victim of circumstances beyond our control that steal away our life, our freedom, our energy, our zeal, our hope, our love. Other times, this force is at work within us, in our egotism, our selfishness, our insecurities and our fears, all the ways our thoughts betray us, withholding compassion and love to ourselves, stirring up all kinds of images and scenarios in our mind that generate anxieties and worry.

Paul is a pastor-theologian. I also hear him as a psychologist, adept in fathoming the depths of the human experience; he knows what lurks and lingers in the human soul and around us and thwarts what we hope and really want. Earlier in chapter 7, Paul writes, "So I find it to be a law that when I want to do what is good, evil lies close at hand. For I delight in the law of God in my inmost self, but I see in my members another law at war with the law of my mind, making me captive to the law of sin that dwells in my members. Wretched man that I am! Who will rescue me from this body of death? Thanks be to God through Jesus Christ our Lord!" (21-25).

Here we begin to see Paul's understanding of the cross, of the incarnation, of why God sent the Son into the world. Listen here: "For God has done what the law, weakened by the flesh, could not do: by sending his own Son in the likeness of sinful flesh, and to deal with sin, he condemned sin in the flesh, so that the just requirement of the law might be fulfilled in us, who walk not according to the flesh but according to the Spirit" (Rom 8: 3-4). In other words, Christ didn't die on the cross in our place; he didn't receive the punishment that we have come to believe we deserve, punishment from a God who is eternally angry with us because our sin. That's not what Paul is saying.

Jesus came to "deal with sin," to "condemn sin in the flesh." In other words, Jesus came to take on the power of sin, the power of the flesh, the power of death, all symbolized by the cross, so that these powers—sin, flesh, death—would no longer enslave and entrap us, that we would be set free, that we would be released from the things that hold us captive. We would then be able to come out from under their oppressive influence, to stand up free, and run in the vast, open space of God's freedom, instead of running around in tight circles in a cage—soul-crushing, life-denying cages.

Paul wants the Romans to know, wants us to know: "There is therefore now no condemnation for those who are in Christ Jesus." One more time: "There is therefore now no condemnation [judgment] for those who are in Christ Jesus." We have been set free. Because to be in Christ, to be baptized in him, to be identified with him, to participate in his life and to have his life in us—

which is what it means to be "in Christ" —means that sin, flesh, and death no longer have the last word in our lives, that we are not ultimately defeated and oppressed by these forces. These forces are still out there, to be sure, but they are no longer definitive for the one who is "in Christ."

Because of what he discovered through Christ, Paul knows there's still another force at work in this universe, another power, another law at work. He encountered it face-to-face on the Damascus Road and in his own life. It's the power of love at work through faith (Gal. 5:6). That's what the resurrection means for Paul—not that when we die we get to go to heaven, but that resurrection itself demonstrates that there is a creative power at work that can bring life out of death and decay and destruction. There is another law that strives to undo the work of sin and death. There's a creative force at work in the world and in us that is stronger than these oppressive forces, stronger than the egotistic self. That force is God and its face is Jesus Christ and the one who continually embodies this force and this person in people and the world is the Holy Spirit.

Between now and the day when death has finally lost its sting and sin is swallowed up in love, we find ourselves in the midst of a cosmic struggle between two "minds": the mind or mentality of the flesh (the attitude, the mind at odds with God) and the mind or mentality of the Spirit, the Spirit who embodied and extends the creative work of Jesus Christ. Paul believed that every person who is in Christ is not ultimately under the domain of the flesh, but under the domain of the Spirit. Indeed, to be in Christ, to be incorporated into him means that the Spirit is influencing us, actually dwelling within us, deep within the depths of our spirits. He wants them to know that there is another law at work in us, the indwelling-life of God's Spirit is within us. It is active and dynamic and powerful and a force to be reckoned with.

In the meantime, how do we know if our lives are being shaped by flesh or Spirit? How can we tell? "For those who live according to the flesh," Paul writes, "set their minds on the things of the flesh, but those who live according to the Spirit, set their minds on the things of the Spirit. To set the mind on the things of the flesh is death, but to set the mind on the Spirit is life and peace."

The Spirit shapes us and molds us by releasing within us the very power, the creativity of God. Not in some, not in isolated religious or spiritual experiences for spiritual elites, but for everyone who is in Christ. For he who raised Christ from the dead is also at work in us to raise us from the dead— not after we die, but here and now. The resurrection is now. It's the kind of life that "breathes the promise of resurrection."[3] The resurrection dwells in us because the Spirit dwells in us. Wherever the Spirit is there is freedom. Wherever the Spirit is, there is life. Wherever the Spirit is, there is peace. To be shaped by the Spirit's mentality is to be called into greater freedom, called out of the cages that entrap us. To be shaped by the Spirit's mentality means that we are continually being called more and more into life, into peace—even in the midst of chaos. These are touchstones, signs, fruits of the Spirit's work in us: freedom, life, peace. These are signs that God is at work in us and doing something with us and through us, activating something new in us—when we embody and exhibit greater freedom, in those places where we are coming alive, when we have a deep sense of peace, confidence, assurance, trust in the work of God in our lives, even in the midst of chaos and confusion.

Where do you see evidence of the mind of the "flesh" in your lives and where do you see manifestations of the mind of the Spirit? Paul tells us that to be in Christ means we already have the mind of the Spirit. But do we? Do you, do we realize this? Do we live from it? Do our life-choices reflect this mentality? What blocks us from realizing this? What causes us to forget who we are? What will it take for us to claim it, to claim who we really are?

A good way to move through these questions is with prayer. An ancient prayer of the church was *Veni Creator Spiritus*. Come, Creator Spirit.[4] It's simple, yet profound. To pray these words is to ask for God's creative presence to fill our lives, to speak to our situation, our circumstances, in our hearts. It's offered with the hope that our minds might be set on the things of the Spirit. *Veni Creator Spiritus*. Come, Creator Spirit. Come.

---

[3] C. E. B. Cranfield, *Romans: A Shorter Commentary* (Grand Rapids: Eerdmans, 1988), 172ff.
[4] Thomas F. Torrance (1913-2007) affirmed, "Come Creator Spirit is a prayer of open surrender to the absolute creativity of God." *Theology in Reconstruction* (London: SCM Press, 1965), 245.

When Jesus Wept

John 11:32-44 & Revelation 21:1-6a

And so we find ourselves in between, caught, as it were, between two tearful texts.

In John 11, we find Jesus summoned to the home of Mary and Martha. Their brother Lazarus was sick and had died and was already in the tomb four days by the time Jesus arrived. Jesus entered a house full of tears. Mary was weeping. Their friends who came to pay their respects were also weeping. Jesus discovered a place flooded with grief and sadness. We're told, as the NRSV renders it, that Jesus "was greatly disturbed in spirit and deeply moved." It's actually stronger in the Greek. "Greatly disturbed in spirit" is really more like *anger*. The Greek verb here describes someone who is furious—even verbally expressing disgust or violent displeasure at something. Groaning, grunting at something. "Deeply moved" is deep emotion, emotion that causes one to shake, to shudder. Shaking and angry, Jesus asked, "Where have you laid him?" "Here, come and see," they said. "Jesus wept." ἐδάκρυσεν ὁ Ἰησοῦς (*edakrysen ho Iēsous*) John 11:35, the shortest verse in the King James Version, should be read this way: "Jesus burst into tears."

In the apocalypse, that is, the revelation given to John the Divine (not the writer of the Gospel, a different John), we find in chapter 21 a glimpse of the vision he saw and an echo of the voice he heard speaking to him. Seeing deep into the mind of God, seeing deep into the future, seeing deep into the end or purpose of history itself, John tells us what he saw:

> Then I saw a new heaven and a new earth ... and I saw the holy city, the new Jerusalem, coming down out of heaven from God ... and I heard a voice from the throne of the Lamb, "See, the home of God is among mortals. He will dwell with them as their God; they will be his peoples, and God himself will be with them; he will wipe every tear from their eyes. Death will be no more; mourning and crying and pain will be no more, for the first things have passed away. (Rev. 21:1-4)

The vision is stunning, staggering in its implications: heaven to earth; earth renewed, not destroyed; God, formerly perceived as distant and aloof will come "down" and in and dwell among us, as God did in Jesus, and will live near us, as close to us as our breath. And God's near-presence will change our lives and remove all that separates us from God and from one another and ourselves. God will wipe every tear from their eyes: mourning and crying and pain will be no more. It's a beautiful sentiment, full of hope. But we must not be sentimental with this text, nor with the reading from John 11. Yes, tears will be wiped dry—completely—which, then, means an end to tears, which, then, means the complete removal of everything that causes us to tear, everything that causes us to mourn and cry, even death itself must be removed.[5] Life-giving water will wash away our tears. For God's presence makes all things new.

And so we find ourselves caught in this in-between time, held, as it were, by these two tearful texts. Jesus bursts out in tears over the death of his friend Lazarus and the promise of a time when tears will cease. But what about us? *How do we, then, live in the meantime?* How do we live until that day when every tear will be removed from our eyes? Let's go back to John's gospel.

Why was Jesus so angry? What bore the brunt of his anger? *Death.* Biblically, theologically speaking, death isn't simply a natural process, a question of biology. We know that it is a natural process, but biblically, theologically speaking it's also something else. And resurrection in the New Testament doesn't necessarily mean the end of biological death, that is, what happens after we physically die. Death is a *force* working against what God intends for us. Death is a *force* that is at odds with God's intention for creation and creatures alike, and what God intends for us is *life*. As I've tried to stress over the years, Koine Greek has two different words for our one English word *life*: *bio*s and *zoe*. *Bio*s is natural life; think of the word *biology*. *Zoe*, on the other hand, is fulfilled life, pregnant with possibility. It's *zoe*, life-giving life, full-life, meaningful life that Jesus offers us, not biology, not simply existing, but being and becoming fully alive! When Jesus said, "I came that they may have life and have it abundantly" (John 10:10), he's talking about *zoe*, not *bio*s. John's gospel calls this *zoe*-life "eternal life," but this doesn't mean life ever after, or life after this life. Instead, "eternal life" in John's gospel (as in John 17:3) is a here-and-now experience; it's really "life touched by eternity," life touched by the divine presence, the life of the everlasting one, namely God; *that's* everlasting life.

How do we know this? It's all over John's gospel, but just focus here on John 11. Jesus raises Lazarus from death. But, think about it. This action didn't stop Lazarus from dying, right? He eventually died. But after his resurrection (that is, the first one) he never lived on earth the same way again—how could he? How can you live life, perceive life the same after you've been brought to true life from out of death? The poet G. K. Chesterton (1874-1936) reflects this radical change of perspective in his poem "The Convert":

---

[5] Brian Blount, *Revelation: A Commentary* (Louisville: Westminster John Knox Press, 2009), 380.

> After one moment when I bowed my head
> And the whole world turned over and came upright
> And I came out where the old road shone white,
> I walked the ways, and heard what all men said...
> They rattle reason out through many a sieve
> That stores the sand and lets the gold go free:
> And all these things are less than dust to me
> Because my name is Lazarus and I live.[6]

The point is this: the everlasting life that Jesus gives is basically the same on both sides of the grave![7] Jesus gives life on both sides of the grave! *This means that we don't have to die in order to know something of Christ's resurrection life.* With Jesus, "Life is changed, not taken away."[8] This also means that until *that day*—when "all shall be well, and all manner of thing shall be well," as the English mystic Julian of Norwich (1342-1416) loved to say—until that day we can be confident that the life of Jesus meets us in our places of pain and torment and suffering, that Jesus' anger rages against all the things, all the forces of death that cause us to weep; he weeps *for* us, he weeps *with* us, and his life-giving presence fills all those places of grief and absence that we know about all too well in our lives. Our tears mixed with his tears. *Our tears, when mixed with his tears, flowing together, can actually become the place we encounter the Lord of Life!* This means we are people—saints!—who witness God's new life in the midst of this dying world; God's resurrection life brings us to life, even in this life marked by tears and pain and sorrow—this is the work of God making all things new! (Rev. 21:5).

At the end of J.R.R. Tolkien's (1892-1973) epic journey *The Lord of the Rings*, in a scene that echoes John's vision in Revelation 21 (Tolkien was a devout Christian, a Roman Catholic), we find the terrible Ring destroyed in the fires of Mount Doom and the world finally free from the evil of Sauron. Now, maybe you love Tolkien; maybe you don't. Maybe you've read *The Hobbit* and *The Lord of the Rings*; maybe you haven't. May you've watched all three movies, including the extended version of each (as I have); maybe you haven't. Nevertheless, the way Tolkien brings his story to a close is amazing.

All those who engaged in the many battles required to free Middle-earth, those that survived, having faced this ordeal of suffering, pain, loss, and death—an ordeal that reflects Tolkien's own experience in the First World War[9]—gather in the woods to honor the Hobbits. Frodo and Sam, the

---

[6] G.K. Chesterton, "The Convert," *The Collected Poems of G. K. Chesterton* (1927).
[7] Gerard Sloyan, *John* (Atlanta: John Knox Press, 1988), 150-151.
[8] Sloyan, 151.
[9] See John Garth, *Tolkien and the Great War: The Threshold of Middle-earth* (Boston: Houghton Mifflin Company, 2003).

heroes, are placed on a throne and everyone bows to them in gratitude. The crowd cheers. A minstrel of Gondor asks to sing a song in praise of "Frodo and ... the Ring of Doom." With tears and laughter, they listened. Here's how Tolkien describes what happens next, "And all the host laughed and wept, and in the midst of their merriment and tears the clear voice of the minstrel rose like silver and gold, and all men were hushed. And he sang to them, now in the [tongue of Elves], now in the speech of the West, until their hearts, wounded with sweet words, overflowed, and their joy was like swords"—that is, pierced by joy— "and they passed in thought out to regions where pain and delight flow together and tears are the very wine of blessedness."[10]

The place "where pain and delight flow together and tears are the very wine of blessedness."

That place is not unlike *this* place, the Table of the Lord, where all our tears of pain and delight flow together with the tears of Christ and become for us the very wine of blessedness.

Blessed Communion.

---

[10] J. R. R. Tolkien, *The Lord of the Rings*: Vol. III – *The Return of the King*, originally published in London by George Allen & Utwin, 1955.

God Gifted

1 Corinthians 12:12-31b

"Now you are the body of Christ," wrote Paul, "and individually members of it" (1 Cor. 12:27). "For just as the body is one and has many members, and all the members of the body, though many, are one body, so it is with Christ" (1 Cor. 12:12).

When Paul considered the church in Corinth this was his image. Many members, one body. One body, many members. It was a body viewed as a whole, with many parts, each indispensable and equal in importance. It's such a beautiful, organic, living, dynamic metaphor for the church of Jesus Christ. We're a *body*. Not a machine. Not a building. Not an institution. Not a business. A *body*.

And not just any body, but the body of *Christ*—the living, breathing body of the once-dead-now-risen body of God's only begotten son.

And not someday, not one day when the church finally gets its act together, not when all the pews are filled and we're exhausted from all the mission we're doing and we have more money than we know what to do with because people are giving in wild abandon—no, not that day. Not then, but *now*.

We're not on the way to becoming the body of Christ. You are, we are, you and I are, right now, the body of the Risen Christ. By virtue of your baptism you have been grafted into the flesh of Christ. This is who you are; this is who we are, together.

This is what Paul wanted the Corinthians to see when they looked at themselves in a mirror. Even if they could only see in that "mirror dimly" (1 Corinthians 13:12), one day they will discover face-to-face and know who they really are and always have been, even when their vision was obscured by a dim mirror.

Paul gives us this vision as a *gift*—and it really is sheer gift. It's a gift that every member of the body is invited to claim and share.

So remember who you are: act, live, breathe like a body. Care for the body. Love the body. Really live *in* this body. Treat the body with the respect it deserves and all its members—*all*—with the honor they deserve. This is what Paul is getting at here.

And it's a truly remarkable affirmation knowing that this church was so divided and full of conflict. Yet, despite its divisions Paul always sees the church as a whole, as *already* possessing a unity found in the "one Spirit" (1 Cor. 12:13). And because this sense of the Spirit is informing how he sees all the members of the church, he invites them to do the same. Claim who you are *already* and live from it, he says. See the unity, the one-ness of the community, because Christ is one. Christ is not divided. Right? And realize that the person right beside you is essential for the work of the Church. All the members are connected, like every member of a body. "If one member suffers," Paul wrote, "all suffer together with it; if one member is honored, all rejoice together" (1 Cor. 12:26).

If we keep reading, chapter twelve pours over into chapter thirteen, the great so-called "love chapter." You know it, "If I speak in the tongues of mortals and of angels, but do not have love, I am a noisy gong or a clanging cymbal. And if I have prophetic powers, and understand all mysteries, all knowledge, and if I have all faith, so as to remove mountains, but do not have love, I am nothing. If I give away all my possessions, and if I hand over my body so that I may boast, but do not have love, I gain nothing. Love is patient; love is kind; love is not envious or boastful or arrogant or rude. It does not insist on its own way; it is not irritable or resentful; it does not rejoice in wrongdoing, but rejoices in the truth. (1 Cor. 13:1-8a).

Chapter 13 is usually read alone, often at weddings; however, chapters 12 and 13 are really one piece, and they should be read together. (I've never attended a wedding in which both chapters were read. Have you?) The reason Paul is writing at length—and beautifully—about love and what love really looks like is because the Corinthians have been fighting and arguing—fighting and arguing over what the church should look like, fighting and arguing over the types of people who should be welcomed there, the forms of worship that should take place there, the kinds of theology that should be preached there, and squabbling over who's going to be in charge, who gets to have the power. As a result, they've forgotten something crucial. They need to remember who they are. They need to remember that they are the body of Christ—which means that they don't belong to themselves.

Without love the members of the body go off on their own, doing their own thing, with their own agendas. Without love all becomes fragmented. Without love one member thinks it's better than the other, instead of seeing how each member is connected to every other member.

Yes, First Church, Corinth was a mess; it was a terribly divided congregation, painfully so. It troubled Paul to no end—and he didn't have the best relationship with them. You can tell how much it weighed on him by the length of this letter, as well as the others he sent to them. There were considerable problems there.

And some of the people in that church needed an attitude adjustment. He refers to them as the *pneumatikoi*, the spiritual ones, so-called, the "spiritual elite," people who thought they were more spiritually gifted than everyone else (see 1 Corinthians 1-3). They saw themselves as "super Christians." It's in this context that Paul wrote, earlier in chapter 12, "Now there are varieties of gifts, but the same Spirit; and there are varieties of services, but the same Lord; and there are varieties of activities, but it is the same God who activates all of them in everyone. To each is given the manifestation of the Spirit for the common good" (1 Cor. 12:4-7). In this light you can begin to see why the only gift that matters is love.

To each is given the manifestation of the Spirit for the common good. Not just some. *To each is given a gift of the Spirit.* Not just some. Everyone—*each*. Each person. Each person in the body of Christ is gifted with at least one gift of the Spirit, probably more. The Spirit has gifted each person who has walked through the waters of baptism. You're probably not the only one to this receive this gift; there could be many in a particular community with the same kinds of gifts. But you definitely have a gift. *You are gifted and talented.*

Gifted and talented.

I remember as a boy that I never liked these words, "gifted and talented." I had friends growing up who were chosen for the Gifted and Talented Program at school. From my perspective as a boy it was all very esoteric. All of a sudden, from out of nowhere, I started hearing about friends who were identified as "special," mysteriously chosen, set apart, invited to take different classes, participate in special programs apart from the rest of us, classes we were not invited to because we were deemed not smart enough or bright enough. Perhaps you were part of the Gifted and Talented Program when you went through school. Perhaps your child is in this program now. I'm sure it's a good program, beneficial in a variety of ways, formative. But from my perspective, someone on the outside, who wasn't in the program, I remember how it made me feel as a boy. I thought and felt inferior, inadequate, that I wasn't gifted, that I wasn't talented—at least not with the gifts and talents others considered worthy of a program. What I had to offer, I thought, had little or no value.

And that's when the seeds of envy were planted in me. They were better than me, and I wanted to be included in that special group. On the plus side, I think at some level the experience motivated me to study hard; it sparked a desire to achieve, to really push myself. *I'll show them!* On the negative side, it sparked a desire to achieve, to strive to at least appear gifted and talented in my teachers' eyes, thus hiding the true gifts and talents embedded in my soul—gifts and talents entrusted to me by the Spirit. I had to discover these later as an adult. That boy is still there in me and he acts up every now and again. But I assure him that he's okay.

Jean Vanier has this to say about *envy*. Vanier is a theologian, humanitarian, and founder of L'Arche Community. Last year he received the prestigious Templeton Prize for his work developing communities, all around the world, for developmentally disabled persons. (If you're not familiar with this work, I highly recommend his books of reflections and essays.[1]) Vanier says, "Envy comes from people's ignorance of, or lack of belief in, their own gifts."[2] This is a beautiful, concise, and accurate description of the origins of envy. Envy surfaces when we're ignorant of our gifts—when we don't know what they are. Or, if known, envy emerges when we lack belief in our gifts—when we don't value them or honor them or trust them. And very often the things we're most envious of in other people are really projections of who we are inside, but for a variety of reasons cannot see or acknowledge as our own.

Many years ago I came across profound wisdom in a statement by Sören Kierkegaard (1813-1855)—that blessed Dane. Kierkegaard has been one of my theological heroes for a long time, a faithful and trusted companion on my journey. (His surname translated into English means, literally, "cemetery"—*kierke*, meaning "church" and *gaard*, meaning "garden" or "yard;" hence, "church yard" or "cemetery." With a name like that you can only imagine what his childhood was like.) With searing psychological and spiritual insight, this is what he said: "Comparison kills." When I first heard those words, many years ago, it was as if the hammer of Thor had struck me, and cracked me open, and released my soul. Kierkegaard said, "The more comparison, the more indolent and paltry a person's life becomes. ... Comparison kills," he said, "with its insidious chill."[3]

He's right. There are healthy forms of comparison, of course. But when we're always comparing ourselves to others—what others have, what others are doing, what others are achieving—if we're always looking outward, valuing what's "out there," more than what's "in here," within us, that which has

---

[1] Jean Vanier, *Community and Growth* (Paulist Press, 1989), 51.
[2] Jean Vanier, *Befriending the Stranger* (Paulist Press, 2010); *From Brokenness to Community* (Paulist Press, 1992); *The Heart of L'Arche: A Spirituality for Every Day* (Novalis, 2012).
[3] Sören Kierkegaard, "Upbuilding Discourses in Various Spirits (1847). The full quote: "... the more comparison, the more indolent and paltry a person's life becomes. This consciousness is the straight gate and the narrow way. It is not the way as such that is narrow, although quite a few people walk along it single-file; no, the narrowness is that each one separately must become the single individual who must press through this narrow pass along the narrow way where no comparison cools, but also where no comparison kills with its insidious chill." *Kierkegaard's Writings*, XV (Princeton: Princeton University Press, 2009), 152.

already been entrusted to us by the Spirit, we are doing ourselves a great disservice and effectively rejecting God's gifts in us. This is not the way toward life, this is not what the Spirit intends for our lives, this is not the way of Christ. Pathological comparison kills: with its insidious chill it slowly, ever so slowly over time kills our souls.

Envy, if left unchecked, has a way of working its wicked way into our souls and then into our relationships and communities. It's a kind of toxin, and it pollutes everything. The congregation in Corinthians was Exhibit A for this. We see it at work today in the Church, in relationships and families, in our communities and places of work.

A more biblical perspective would have better served me as a boy. To be in the body of Christ means I am gifted and talented. If you're in the body of Christ, then you are gifted and talented. Your gifts and your talents don't make you better than anyone else. We're all the same in the eyes of God—equally loved. Whatever gifts or talents I have or you have are not given for your sake alone and not because you're better than anyone else. We are gifted in order to share our gifts with others. The Spirit has gifted us each in a unique and particular way, so that our gifts can be used for the common good. We're not allowed to hoard them or protect them. We're not allowed not to use them. The gifts are to be shared. They're given to us so that we can give them to the world—it's one of the ways God acts in the world through us. By virtue of our baptism, God blesses us with abilities and capacities that can, quite literally, transform the world. Perhaps that's why there's sometimes a reluctance to accept our gifts and talents, because then we're responsible for them and have to do something with them. And this probably frightens us.

What are yours gifts? Are you using them? If not, why not? What are you afraid of? What's holding you back?

What are our gifts as a church? Are we using them? If not, why not? What are we afraid of? What's holding us back?

Do you not know? Have you not heard? "You *are* the body of Christ." *Now.* "Now you are the body of Christ." *Thanks be to God!*

Life-Giver

Acts 2:1-21
Pentecost

I often wonder why Pentecost doesn't have the same fascination, the same amount of celebration as Christmas and Easter. We've all heard of C & E Christians—Christmas and Easter Christians—you might even know one or two. But have you ever met a C, E, & P Christian? I don't think so. We don't have to set up extra chairs in the sanctuary on Pentecost, as we did on Easter this year. We don't have packed pews this morning as we had on Christmas Eve. No brass quartets. No Pentecost carols. No one has ever complained to me that we didn't sing enough Pentecost hymns leading up to today—not that there are that many to choose from. No Pentecost bonnets or candy for the day. There are no Hallmark cards to mark the occasion. So, where are you going for Pentecost brunch after worship today?

Given the theological weight of Christmas—Annunciations, Incarnation, "God with us," and the "Word became flesh and dwelt among us, full of grace and truth"—and the profundity of Easter—death and resurrection, empty tombs, garden encounters with the Risen Christ—it's tough to compete with these two events. Not that it's a competition, of course. But Pentecost has never measured up against these two days. All that I remember about Pentecost as a child is that it was the day we had a delicious buttercream sheet cake during fellowship hour that read "Happy Birthday" to the Church. That was my earliest association with the day. But it didn't measure up against Christmas and Easter. Pentecost is the day we celebrate the birth of the church. That is the way Luke describes it here in Acts 2. The formation of the church is worth celebrating, of course, but Pentecost has never really obtained "big religious holiday" status.

Perhaps this is because Pentecost has to do with arrival of the Holy Spirit, and the Church has never known what to "do" with the Holy Spirit. She's often cast aside as the orphan of the Trinity, the "third-wheel." The early Church theologians insisted that the Holy Spirit is one of the "persons" of the Trinity, equal to the other two, sharing the same essence. Yet many Christians who claim to believe in the Trinity are really Binatarians, who worship God and Jesus and ignore the active, dynamic presence of the Spirit.

This brings me back to my quandary about Pentecost. At times I think we should elevate Pentecost *above* Christmas and Easter—a little loopy, I know, maybe even heretical, but hear me out.

By Pentecost I mean *not* the formation of the Church, but the unleashing of the Holy Spirit upon the world. Now, whether the Holy Spirit arrived in Jerusalem after Jesus' ascension, as we have here in Acts 2, or, whether she arrived on Easter when Jesus breathed his Resurrection Spirit into the disciples, as we read in John 20, is the beside the point. They both point to the fact that something happened, that the presence, power, and purpose of the Holy Spirit were given to disciples to equip and empower and direct them for Christ's ongoing work in the world. The Spirit was unleashed upon the world, blowing as a gentle breeze to comfort fearful disciples, assuring them of Christ's ongoing presence, or, raging as a forceful, violent tempest to challenge, disturb, and ultimately thrust disciples beyond the confines of an upper room, locked away by fear, sent out beyond Jerusalem to a world waiting to hear the gospel, sent out to introduce the world to the presence of the Risen Christ.

You see, the Holy Spirit makes Christ present to us. The Holy Spirit presents us with the very life of Christ. The Spirit is the life-giver, the giver of resurrection, who brings new life to the dead parts of our lives, and, ultimately brings us into the presence of the Resurrected One at the end of our days.

The Holy Spirit is the *fons vitae*, as John Calvin (1509-1564) liked to say, the fountain of life. The Spirit makes Christ real. The Spirit makes the gospel real. The Spirit gives us faith. The Spirit allows us to confess our faith.

The Spirit conveys the love of God. The Holy Spirit whispers to the depths of our spirits and reminds us again and again that we are beloved children of grace, children of the covenant, bound to God.

The Spirit extends Christ to us so that we know that "God is with us." The Spirit comforts and assures us, gives us strength when we are weak, calms our nerves when we're afraid and anxious.

The Spirit is an *agent provocateur* who pokes and prods and pushes us to grow and to *grow up* into the image of God in Christ. The Spirit is continually working within the depths of the psyche in order to yield *life* for us,
true life,
abundant life,
hopeful life,
meaningful life,
God-praising, Christ-serving, sacrificial life,
a life that is even willing to suffer for the sake of God's love.

The Spirit, as Paul knew, plumbs the depths of our spirits and prays *for* us, prays *with* us, even when we don't have the words to pray (Rom. 8:25). The Spirit groans *with* us—*groans!*—groans *for* us, as Paul says, with sighs too deep for words (Romans 8:26).

You see, the Spirit translates for us—we who were untimely born, living more than twenty centuries after Jesus—the meaning, the power, the presence of his life, death, and resurrection. For without the work of the Holy Spirit, Jesus' life, death, and resurrection are merely events that occurred a long time ago, historical "facts," something we "believe" occurred in the past that we remember or commemorate. Jesus and his message then become distant, instead of something, someone close to us, that we experience here and now.

Kevin Kling, playwright and storyteller, recently said at the Festival of Homiletics in Minneapolis, "There was a time when the Bible had a skin cover and floated on the breath of spoken words." He's right. There was a time when we didn't need the Bible, as heretical as this might sound, because the Spirit was alive within Christ's followers, in their *experience*.

The Lutheran theologian Regin Prenter (1907-1990) made this clear in his classic work *Spiritus Creator*. He said, "The Spirit is the real, divine sphere in which Christ comes out of the remoteness of history and the realm of pure ideas and becomes living, present reality—becomes *experience*."[4] The Holy Spirit gives us an actual *experience* of Christ.

Long before Prenter it was John Calvin (1509-1564) who spoke eloquently and provocatively about the person and work of the Spirit. "Till our minds are fixed on the Spirit," Calvin said, "Christ remains of no value to us; because we look at [Christ] as an object of cold speculation without us, [that is, outside us], and therefore at a great distance from us." Without the Spirit, Calvin insists, Christ is far removed from us, buried in a remote past, someone we view remotely, objectively, cold, a "fact" of history to be studied and learned about, instead of a Christ encountered, a present reality, Christ known, Christ with us and for us and within us. Calvin insists, "It is only by his Spirit that he unites himself with us; and by the grace and power of the same Spirit we are made his members," so that "we may mutually enjoy him."[5]

---

[4] Regin Prenter, *Spiritus Creator*, trans. John M. Jensen (Eugene, OR: Wipf and Stock, 2000 [1946]), 198-199.
[5] John Calvin, *Institutes of the Christian Religion* (1559), II.i.3.

And because we are in relationship with the Risen Christ, through the Spirit, the Spirit of the Risen Christ extends resurrection to us. The Holy Spirit raises us up from our own personal tombs of death and decay, all the places we are dead or stuck.

The Holy Spirit is power, fire, energy, vital and vitalizing.
The Holy Spirit is dynamic, moving, swift and invisible,
like the wind, a wind—sometimes gentle, sometimes fierce—
trying
to bring us to life,
to animate our souls,
to move our feet forward,
to get us to stretch out our hands in service, mission, and witness,
to cause our hearts to beat faster with joy.

It's only when the Holy Spirit is giving life to us that we can say the Spirit is bringing life to the Church. A Church that God is trying to take some place, moving us along, empowering us and inspiring us to be the people of God.

It's been said that the Church is dying. Perhaps it is. Some say Christianity is dying. Perhaps it is. Its message doesn't seem to connect with folks the way it used to. The way the Church perceives itself is definitely changing. Christianity is changing. Change is inevitable, it's natural. We can resist the change—which the Church loves to do. Or, maybe—just maybe—the change we're experiencing is actually a sign that the Holy Spirit is at work in us, reforming us. That's what I think, primarily because I trust in the movement of the Spirit. The Spirit doesn't want to take us back to the past but to propel us forward into God's future.

I was reminded of this recently. Over the past six months the driver side mirror on my Jetta was knocked off, ripped right off. Not once, not twice, but three times. The first time occurred in December, in front of my house; it was clipped by a snow plow that drove too close and smashed the mirror. The second time occurred right here in front of the Church House on Beechwood Avenue. Hit and run. This time the fender was dented, the mirror shattered. And the third time occurred two weeks later, also on Beechwood Avenue, same location. This time the person left a note. I don't park there anymore. Was there a message in all of this for me? It's easy to go crazy trying to read meaning into events, but perhaps all of these incidents were trying to say to me: *stop looking back*. Look ahead. Drive forward. The Spirit propels us forward, into tomorrow, into the future.

The Spirit wants to move us. That's why it's important to remember that God is a *verb* and not a noun; this distinction makes a considerable difference in our lives. A verb implies movement, action. A noun is an object. It doesn't move. The God revealed to us on Sinai is a verb. God said to Moses, my name is: I AM. Yahweh. *I am who I am; I will be who I will be* (Exodus 3:14). Being itself. Jesus Christ and the Spirit share the same dynamic life of God and offer that life to us. Yet it's so easy to see them as nouns, instead of verbs. Jesus, *Yeshua*, means "Yahweh saves," and the Spirit, *pneuma* in Greek, means "breath" and "wind." They both imply movement.

My friend James Hollis, a Jungian analyst, suggests that we would be better served by transforming some of our nouns to verbs. It might make for "inelegant English," but we would be better off. We need to think of the human self, for example, not as a noun, but as a verb: a self *selfing*. Our stories are *storying* us. Nature is *naturing;* it's not static. Hollis says, "Our ego, in service to understanding and the need for control converts the elemental processes in life into nouns. We foolishly convert even 'the gods' into nouns, into objects 'up there,' looking down, rather than metaphors" for something at work in us and through us.[6] When we turn verbs into nouns we fixate them, stop their movement or development or change or transformation, we grab hold of them and control them. We do the same with our images of God; we're often guilty of turning a verb into a noun, into a static idol. "We turn the mystery into nouns and make them objects."[7]

Perhaps, this, too, is why the Church has been reluctant to embrace the work of the Spirit, because the Spirit is pure verb: movement, action, blowing wherever she will, beyond our control—*and that scares us*. And it should! But fear not!

What if we faced that fear and let ourselves go? What if we opened the sails of our spirits and allowed the Holy Spirit to blow through our lives in new ways, moving us forward, carrying us wherever we need to go? What would happen to us? What would happen to the Church? I don't know for sure. But what I do know is that it will take the form of Christ: his grace, his joy, his goodness, his suffering-love, taking on flesh in our lives in tangible, life-changing, transforming ways. It will be a church—a people—alive and always coming alive! *Come, Holy Spirit! Come!*

---

[6] James Hollis, *Hauntings: Dispelling the Ghosts Who Run Our Lives* (Ashville, NC: Chiron Publications, 2013), 1-2, 30. Hollis is making a psychological point here, not a theological one, but it's equally relevant.
[7] James Hollis in a talk given to the Jung Society of Washington, Embassy of Switzerland, Washington, DC, 7th June 2014.

Unlocking the Doors of Fear

John 20:19-31

Two Sundays ago, on Easter, we read from John 20 and heard the story of Jesus near the tomb, disguised as the gardener. Jesus reached out to Mary Magdalene in her grief, saying, "Woman, why are you weeping? Whom are you looking for?" (John 20:15). Jesus told her not to hold on to him because he was about to ascend to the Father.

Then, later that same day, "the evening on that day," John tells us, "the first day of the week" (Jn. 20:19), which we call Sunday, we find the disciples behind locked doors. They are back in the house where they gathered before Jesus' death; perhaps the site of their last supper together. John tells us, "and the doors of the house where the disciples had met were locked for fear of the Jews, Jesus came and stood among them and said, 'Peace be with you'" (Jn. 20:19).

This, too, is a remarkable scene that we have in John's gospel: Jesus' astonishing exchange with the disciples locked away in fear. *"The doors of the house ... were locked for fear."* That's such an evocative phrase and image.

In phrasing it this way, I'm intentionally omitting the object of their fear—"the Jews." I'm doing this for two reasons. First, the reference to "the Jews" in John's gospel has inflicted considerable damage and violence toward the Jewish people. Scholars have identified John's gospel as one of the major sources of anti-Semitism. In fact, we Christians need to remember our role in the propagation of anti-Semitism across the centuries. We need to remember that the Nazis, for example, did not invent the concept of the Jewish ghetto. (Think of the Warsaw ghetto.) The Nazis got the idea from Christians.

I was surprised to discover years ago that Venice, Italy, was the site of the first Jewish ghetto, in 1516. It was the only place Jews were allowed to live in the city. And I was surprised to discover there was also a Jewish ghetto in Rome (the Ghetto di Roma), built in 1555, surrounded by walls, with three gates and a Vatican guard that made sure no Jew left the area after dark.[1]

---

[1] Papal bull *Cum nimis absurdum*, promulgated by Pope Paul IV in 1555, segregated the Jews, who had lived freely in Rome since Antiquity, and subjected them to various restrictions on their personal freedoms such as limits to allowed professions and compulsory hearing of Catholic sermons on the Jewish Shabbat.

John's attitude toward "the Jews" of Jesus' time has been used to justify Christian pogroms against all Jews across the centuries. However, biblical scholars now suspect that John's use of "the Jews" throughout the gospel is really a code word for the Jewish religious establishment. He's not referring to *everyone* who is Jewish (which would include both John and Jesus, who were, of course, both Jewish).

The second reason for omitting "the Jews" here allows us, we who are not necessarily fearful of "the Jews," to access the depth of meaning of a text like this. While we might not be afraid of "the Jews," we are certainly people who know what it's like to live with fear. *"The doors of the house ... were locked for fear."*

The disciples are hiding; scared for their lives. Why? The text doesn't say, but it's not difficult to imagine multiple scenarios. They're afraid of being persecuted for following the "criminal" Jesus. They are marked men. Perhaps they're fearful of retaliation. If Jesus wasn't alive, then they would be attacked for being associated with the blasphemer who claimed to be God's Son and stirred up the city and annoyed the Roman authorities. We can imagine them trying to find a way to get out of Jerusalem, to flee to safety in Galilee.

No doubt news was spreading about what happened at the garden tomb. But why would this invoke fear? Think about it. If it's true, if resurrection is true, then it's kind of difficult to return to life as "normal" after that. Resurrection changes everything. If Jesus is alive, then their commitment to him would be even stronger than it was when he was alive (which wasn't all that strong). And so they can't just set aside the whole experience with Jesus as a kind of bad dream and then go back to life as normal; they can't go home again. There's no going back to "normal." If Jesus is alive, then this really does change *everything*. And in the face of such radical change, it is easy to imagine the disciples huddled together in fear behind locked doors—that's probably where I would have been.

We can't blame them for being fearful. On the one hand, fear was probably the appropriate and natural reaction to all that they experienced. If they weren't fearful, then they probably weren't paying attention to what was going on around them that weekend in Jerusalem. Fear is the normal, rational response when one feels threatened, attacked, unsure, confused.

Fear is such a powerful emotion, with both positive and negative dimensions to it. There's a lot about fear that is good. There are rational fears that serve an evolutionary function, which have allowed humans to survive for millennia. Fear can be a good defense mechanism against all kinds of predators. There's something primal about the way fear can be used as a way to keep us safe. When we're fearful we respond with whatever it takes to keep us safe; it motivates us toward security. Feeling safe and secure are good things, obviously. It's impossible to live and thrive without security, without a feeling of being safe.

Sometimes fear is a perfectly rational response—but if we get stuck there, stuck in the fear, then that becomes a source of considerable concern. That's when fear can become the prison of the heart.

Fear—throughout scripture—never has the final word in any scenario. It's never lifted up as being the permanent state of being for God's children. We are not called to live in fear, but in freedom, including freedom from fear. Whenever the disciples are afraid, the voice of the angels or the voice of Jesus himself—the voice of God—is always consistent: "Fear not." "Do not be afraid." Over and over again, the good news of the kingdom is "Fear not." Don't live your lives in fear. Instead live your lives with love. And the New Testament is the only text I've ever read that states explicitly that the opposite of love is not *hate*; the opposite of love is *fear*. As we read in 1 John 4:18, "There is no fear in love, but perfect love casts out fear." And it's when we fear that we then hate and attack and persecute and destroy and murder and kill.

Years ago, a wise ruling elder said to me, "Ken, we act either in love or fear." We have two choices. We can choose to act either in love or fear. At first, I was a little suspicious, thinking that it's not that simple. But she was right. It might sound overly simplistic, but I think it's true. Just look over your life. Consider the countless decisions you make on any given day or week or over a lifetime—are they, were they done in fear or in love? Think of the major decisions you have made in your life or decisions that need to be made. Love or fear? Which will dictate your life? Which governs your life?

The truth is there are so many places in our lives, in the church, in the world that are not governed by love, but fear. The truth is there are so many places in our lives, in the church, in the world today being destroyed by fear. The more you become aware of it, the more you see it everywhere. In addition to fear, there's the related emotion of anxiety. We all know the price we pay when children are raised to be fearful and anxious, they tend to be apprehensive. If children are raised in environments that are fearful, they become defensive. Back in 1959, Dorothy Law Nolte (1924-2005) wrote a poem that became well-known, "Children Learn What They Live." It begins with these lines, "If a child lives with criticism, he learns to condemn ... / If a child lives with hostility, he learns to fight ... / If a child lives with fear, he learns to be apprehensive." The poem continues with a description of what is learned when a child lives with acceptance, tolerance, justice, approval.[2] My

---

[2] The complete text may be found here:
http://www.empowermentresources.com/info2/childrenlearn-long_version.html.

mother had a copy of this poem, the 1969 version, on the wall of the bedroom that I shared with my brother Craig. I remember reading those lines over and over again as boy.

Children are growing up and maturing in a world overwhelmed by the presence of fear. The world can be a fearful place for a child. It's probably always been the case. But earlier generations were raised in communities that shared a common religious perspective, one that provided considerable resources for children. There was a time when family and community, religious communities in particular, helped provide a secure, safe place for growth. This is completely missing for many today.

The source of so much hatred in our society is rooted in fear. The specter of racism that is raising its ugly head again in the United States is rooted in fear of the other. The rising intolerance for anyone or anything that doesn't fit the "norm" is rooted in fear. Society is changing; the church is changing. (And not all of this is bad. A lot of it is very, very good.) But too much change too fast produces anxiety. Sometimes our resistance to change is simply rooted in fear. The rise of Christian, Jewish, and Islamic fundamentalisms over the last century, especially over the last decade, each have one thing in common: *fear*. Christian fundamentalism emerged as a movement in the early 1900s, here in the United States, as a fearful reaction to advances made in science and learning. We then gave this fear to the world.[3]

God doesn't want our lives governed by fear. Again, fear might have an evolutionary function that allows us to survive; however, theologically and psychologically speaking, we know that fear can suck the life out of us and actually hinder our ability to thrive. When fear generates an obsession with safety and security—when we're always living behind locked doors—then we cut ourselves off from life itself. The Swiss psychiatrist, Carl G. Jung (1875-1961), observed "negation of the life force by fear" is "the spirit of evil." Only boldness can deliver us from fear, and if the risk is not taken, the meaning of life is violated.[4] James Hollis, a contemporary Jungian analyst, builds on this point, "The meaning of our life will be found precisely in our capacity to achieve as much of it as possible beyond those bounds fear would set for us. There is no blame in being fearful; it is our common lot, our common susceptibility. But it may be a crime, an impiety ..., when our individual summons, our destiny, is diverted or destroyed by fear."[5] This is a

---

[3] See George M. Marsden, *Fundamentalism and American Culture: The Shaping of Twentieth-Century Evangelicalism: 1870-1925* (Oxford: Oxford University Press, 1980).
[4] C. G. Jung, *Symbols of Transformation*, The Collected Works of C. G. Jung, Vol. 5 (Princeton: Princeton University Press, 1967), §551.
[5] James Hollis, *What Matters Most: Living a More Considered Life* (New York: Gotham Books, 2009), 15.

remarkable insight: life governed by fear as an impiety, an expression of being faithless.

It's precisely in such a context that we hear Jesus' words to his disciples. God will not allow fear to have the last word. In fear the disciples try to hide themselves from a world that resists all the implications of the life-changing, liberating power of resurrection. But fear can't hinder the new life Jesus extends to us! Resurrection life acknowledges the fear, but it does not allow the fear to divert or destroy what God is doing through Jesus and through us. We're given a truly remarkable image here. I love the way the resurrected Jesus appears within the locked room and stands among them there; he stands within the confines of their fear; he appears and stands in their place of greatest fear and says, "Peace be with you." Even locked doors can't keep him out. Christ's boldness overcomes every barrier we try to erect in fear. We're not meant to live behind locked doors. Within the confines of all our fears, Jesus continues to stand among us, unlocking our prisons of fear, and saying, "Peace be with you."

The place of fear can become the place of presence, the place of peace, the place of resurrection. The text tells us that their fear was replaced with rejoicing at the sight of his presence. That's what resurrection can do. That's what the resurrected Lord continues to do.

And, did you notice how these verses contain John's version of Pentecost? There are no "tongues of fire," as we find in Acts. What we have here is Jesus saying, "Peace be with you. As the Father has sent me, so I send you." Sent to be agents of peace, agents of his presence, offering assurance in every other fearful place we find in the world. Then Jesus breathed on them and said, "Receive the Holy Spirit" (Jn. 20:22).

In that place where you hide, locked away in fear, Jesus still says,
"Peace be with you."

In all that instills fear in you, Jesus still says,
"Peace be with you."

In the prison of the heart bound by fear, Jesus still says,
"Peace be with you."

In the lives of people, we know who are overwhelmed by fear,
the Lord sends us to say in his name,
"Peace be with you."

In a world ensnared by fear the Lord sends
the Church out to offer a different voice to the world, saying,
"Peace be with you."

Every place where we are tempted to act in fear over love,
may we remember the words of the Risen Lord
who said and continues to say to us:
"Peace be with you."
"Peace be with you."
"Peace be with you."
"Peace."

Removing Every Tear

Isaiah 25:6-9 & Revelation 21:1-6a
All Saints' Day

I was recently asked, "Where have you suffered?" The question took me aback and knocked me off-guard. It was asked by someone whom I really didn't know very well, and so I was reluctant to respond from the heart. For this is a heart, a soul question.

I thought about it and answered: I have suffered most in my losses. In saying this, I can think of plenty of people I know whose losses have been significantly greater than mine. Comparatively speaking, I guess, some might say my losses are manageable (and to a considerable extent they are). But they are nevertheless mine, as yours are yours.

In my life, I've had to say good-bye to far too many very dear family members and close friends. I was born almost three months to the day of my maternal grandfather's death. My mother was carrying me when she said good-bye to her father. I entered into a household full of mourning and loss. Years later as a boy, I remember feeling the loss, especially around holidays. I became aware, very early, earlier than I should have, that life is precarious and that death is never far away. I've always had an existential bent; life is serious and important and fragile. I came aware of my own finitude at an early age. (This is probably why I tend to be pretty serious at times.) When I was in fifth grade I lost a classmate to cancer and then my fifth grade math teacher died. I lost uncles to whom I was very close when I was in sixth grade. A mentor friend died when I was in high school, Jim Loebell. My mother, Grace, died at 59 in 1992; her mother, Ann, died in 2000. In the opening pages of my doctoral dissertation there's dedicatory page to all the people I lost along the way in the writing of the thesis. I've had a lot of personal loss. Add to the loss all the people I've come to know and love as a pastor for twenty years. On All Saints' Day I think of them and see their faces.

You have your memorial list. You have the names and faces of people who have gone on before you. The longer we live, the longer the list. Sometimes human grief is overwhelming. The tears just keep on flowing. "Time heals all wounds" is a lie. For many the wounds are raw and real. Most folks work through their grief in healthy ways, but many don't. Most folks find a way to carry on, but many don't. Many suffer silently. They offer prayers to God with groans too deep for words. And the tears just keep on flowing.

We grieve for our losses. We grieve for our neighbor's losses. We grieve for a world that is drenched with tears. That's what we do in the church. We don't advertise ourselves this way. We don't have, "Come and grieve with us," out on the Frederick Road sign. But this is what we do. Where else can people go with their grief, their sorrow? Where else can it be held by a community with love and care? If we're not grieving in one way or the other, we're probably not paying attention—to the tears of the world, to tears of our neighbors and friends and loved ones, of the silent tears of our hearts.

Jesus said, "Blessed are those who mourn, for they shall be comforted" (Matthew 5:4). *Happy*, exceedingly happy are those who mourn. Happy, blessed is the one who can grieve. In his translation of the New Testament from Greek into German, Martin Luther (1483-1546) translated "mourn" with *Leidtragen*, meaning "sorrow-bearing." It's an odd blessing, until we realize that what Jesus was getting at was this: blessed is the one who bears the sorrows of the world and neighbor and self, because those who mourn have God's ear—and they will be comforted.[1]

In Isaiah 25, we heard God's promise that there will come a day when all will be put to right. "On this mountain Yahweh will make for all peoples a feast of rich food, a feast of well-aged wines, of rich food filled with marrow, of well-aged wines strained clear. And Yahweh will destroy on this mountain the shroud—the funeral pall—that is cast over all peoples.... Then Yahweh will wipe away the tears from all faces.." That's Isaiah's vision for the time to come. It is powerful, confident in the identity and purpose of God, a God who does not intend God's people to suffer and mourn and cry, but to sit at a feast of rich food.

Centuries later, the Holy Spirit gave a revelation to John on the Island of Patmos. In that vision he saw way into the future and like Isaiah received a glimpse into the future God will bring about, of a promise fulfilled. "See, the home of God is among mortals. He will dwell with them as their God; they will be his peoples, and God himself will be with them; he will wipe every tear from their eyes. Death will be no more; mourning and crying and pain will be no more, for the first things have passed away. ...Behold, Jesus says to John, "I am making all things new. ...I am the Alpha and the Omega, the beginning and the end." In other words, all of time is wrapped up in him, the Resurrected One. In him all the peoples of the world will find their rest. In time, there will come a time when everything lost will be restored and made new again. In him, there is a hope that despite the pain and sorrow and

---

[1] Dietrich Bonhoeffer, *The Cost of Discipleship* (New York: Collier Books, 1963[1937]), 121. "For the emphasis lies on the bearing of sorrow. The disciple-community does not shake off sorrow as though it were no concern of its own, but willingly bears it. And in this way they show how close are the bonds which bind them to the rest of humanity." (121-122).

suffering and loss of our lives, the pain and sorrow and suffering and loss never – *never!* – have the last word.

As a Minister of Word and Sacrament, as Christian, as a human being who has felt the sting of death, I wish I never had to do another funeral again. But I'll tell you there is no greater privilege in being a minister than standing with a family in the throes of grief and loss, in the intimacy of those places—seeing things, hearing things, experiencing things most people will never see or hear or know. I know Dorothy Boulton shares this view. And there's no greater joy than to stand in this pulpit or sit at a bedside and declare the gospel, to read from Revelation 21 with conviction and assurance and give witness to the power of the resurrection—*because if it's not true in those heart-wrenching moments then it isn't true in any other moment.* I don't say this because you pay me to, because I'm a minister, but because experience yields conviction and conviction demands faithfulness. It's what I've come to know in and through my suffering.

How can I say all of this? Only because of *grace*. The gospel is true. Something happens when we gather as a community around those we love with the love and support and grace of Christ. It's what makes the church so unique. There's no place like it. This is the place where we hold each other's sorrow and grief. When we *share* our sorrows and our grief, Christ is present there. The cross stands at the heart of all that we do, and there's no getting around it. Christ's message from the cross says to us: *in your suffering you're not alone. In your suffering you'll find me. In your losses I am present because I am greater than death.*

On this All Saints' Day, we are reminded of our losses. It's a heavy day; this is a heavy sermon, intentionally so. It's sobering—not meant to be grim, but to be real, honest. It's an invitation for us as a church to share our sorrow, to carry one another along in our losses and grief. There's an old Egyptian proverb that goes, "Be kind. Everyone is fighting a hard battle." We are all broken. We all know loss. But we are given the gift of one another so that as a church—with saints above and saints below—we can share our sorrow; and when we do, we soon discover Christ's presence among and within us.

Christ showed us that we experience God's grace in the broken places, in the sorrowful, tearful, crying places. Why does it have to be this way? I haven't a clue: that's the way it is. God's grace is known the strongest in the weak and hurting and broken places—which is precisely the point of this Table and the celebration of the Lord's Supper and why he invites us to share this meal. Here we remember our loss of him but also how he was known to us in the breaking of the bread (Luke 24:35). But it has to be broken and then shared; then the meal takes on life, the life of Jesus who was broken for us and shared his life. It has to be broken and then shared; when lives break, when broken lives share, Jesus promises to be there too. An unwillingness to be broken and to share means we miss the Christ.

A friend of mine tells the story of a church with a lot of customs and traditions, and they didn't like anybody disrupting them. The church had an interim minister who was trying to shake things up a bit but wasn't being too successful. This church had the custom of putting a loaf of bread on a communion plate on the table every week. They don't celebrate the Lord's Supper every week, but they have a symbol of the sacrament. If you think that would be expensive or wasteful to have an unused loaf of bread on the Communion table every week, don't worry. They use the same loaf. It is a large unsliced loaf of Italian bread covered with polyurethane. So they use the same bread over and over again. One Sunday the minster was leading people in Communion. He lifted the ceremonial loaf of bread, said, "Take eat, this is my body." Then he cracked it open and ripped it apart.

There was a collective gasp in the congregation. Then it was absolutely silent as he continued to break the bread into large chunks to place on the Communion trays. It took a few minutes for people to realize the minister had switched the polyurethane bread with a real loaf. Afterward, someone said, "You really had us going there for a minute. We thought you actually broke our Communion bread."

The minister said, "If it isn't broken, it can't be shared."[2]

On this Sunday we acknowledge our losses—all the broken, hurting places in our lives—and we share them, in and through this meal. As we do we will find the Risen Christ because that's where he is known to us, in our losses.

"O blest Communion, fellowship divine. We feebly struggle, they glory shine. Yet all are one in Thee for all are Thine. Alleluia! Alleluia!"[3]

---

[2] Sermon by William G. Carter, "If There Isn't Enough to Go Around," William G. Carter, ed. *Speaking of Stewardship: Model Sermons on Money and Possessions* (Louisville: Geneva Press, 1989), 117-118.
[3] William W. How, "For All the Saints" (1864).

Finding Your Way Home

Luke 15:1-10 & 1 Timothy 1:12-17

No one likes getting lost. I know I don't. One of my first memories of getting lost was when I was around five years old. It took place at a department store in Kearny, New Jersey, called Two Guys (once a small store chain in Northern New Jersey). I was there with my mother, Grace, and my brother, Craig. Somehow, I don't remember how, I got separated from them. What I do remember is sitting on the customer service counter, which was located on the first floor, in the center of the store, and that I crying and very worried. I was scared. Eventually my mother showed up with Craig in-tow. She reached out to me, I reached out to her, and I cried all the more. That really shook me up. It took me a while to calm down. I think we stopped to get some ice cream before making our way home. My mother always knew what to do.

It's not fun getting lost, especially having all the associated feelings that come with lost*ness*. Feeling separated, feeling abandoned, cut off, alone.

One time I abandoned someone. Unintentionally, but it happened. It was the first tour of Scotland I led back in 1996. We had 35 in our group. We were on the Isle of Skye, way up in the north. We had stopped for a tour of the Clan Donald Centre, on the south end of the island, and then headed north to Kyle of Lochalsh, back on the mainland where we were to spend the night. When I lead tours, I always have the group count-off before the bus pulls away from a stop (much to the consternation and frustration of the group). One time we didn't count, we drove off. Soon, someone asked, "Where's Madeleine?" We thought she was in the rest room on the bus. But she wasn't. Twenty minutes *en route* we had to turn the large bus around on a very narrow single-track road we were on, using a farm lane to do a K-turn, and then headed back to collect her. She was sitting there in the parking lot, alone. The bus stopped, I ran out, wrapped my arms around her and said, "Madeleine, I'm *so* sorry!" She laughed. She didn't seem too concerned. She said, "No worries, Ken. As a mother of nine, I'm used to leaving one of my kids behind." That's the last time I left someone behind on a tour (at least I think I so).

No one likes getting lost. With GPS systems in our cars and Smartphones and the use of MapQuest or Google Maps, fewer of us run the chance of getting lost these days. I wonder, though, if people are losing the ability to read maps. They just go wherever OnStar sends them.

But sometimes we do get lost. Lost, not on the way to the Columbia Mall or to Costco, but lost in terms of purpose, direction, and meaning. Increasingly, I sense that there are more and more people who are wandering aimlessly through life, not really clear about who they are or what they feel called to do. With the crisis of contemporary Christianity upon us, with fewer people going to church, or practicing any faith, so many turn to other things to fill the cravings of their soul: materialism, careerism, consumerism. Thinking we can shop our way toward meaning, or that things will make us happy, or work our way toward purpose, or medicate our way out of the anxiety of life through addictions. The signs are everywhere, we have lost our moorings and we're set adrift.

It might seem that it's worse today than ever before. Each generation, I think, feels it was better in an earlier time. Sometimes that's true. What's clear though is that this feeling of being lost, of searching and wandering in a world coming unhinged is not new to human experience. It's universal. In fact, it's part of the human condition. It's been with us for a very long time. Poets and prophets are usually the ones who are in touch with these feelings. The poet John Donne (1572-1631) wrote:

> Tis all in pieces
> all coherence gone. ("An Anatomy of the World")

Several centuries later, William Butler Yeats (1865-1939) wrote:

> Turning and turning in the widening gyre,
> The falcon cannot hear the falconer.
> Things fall apart; the centre cannot hold;
> Mere anarchy is loosed upon the world. ("The Second Coming")

Perhaps it feels like things are falling apart, that's things don't make any sense, that we're set adrift and lost, because we have a deeper memory or deeper feeling that there was a time when we were whole, when things made sense, when we felt at home.

When I speak of being lost, I don't mean in a metaphysical sense, that is lost to God, the opposite of being "saved." I know plenty of Christians who trust in Jesus who yet feel lost and confused. While they were "once lost, but now found" by grace, it doesn't mean that they know where they are or where they're going.

For the truth is, there are times, even as faithful Christians, when we lose our way. We forget who we are and whose we are and we fall, fall away from ourselves, fall away from God, fall away from the things that matter most. There are times when life becomes so overwhelming and complex or times when everything is going so well, that we start to stray from the straight and narrow path; we lose our way, lose our footing, and begin to wander away from who we are, wander away from God, wander away from the things that give us life and meaning and purpose. It happens.

If we wander away for too long, go down other paths, take detours, get stuck in cul-de-sacs, it's difficult making our way home, back to our true selves, back to God, back to a life of meaning. What happens then is that we settle for living with falsehoods and falsity, in service to false and lesser selves; we know we miss that relationship with God that we had at one time; we remember those former times, but we've been away for so long it feels impossible to go back, perhaps tempted by false gods and meaningless, mindless ways of living, and we forget the way back.

The Pharisees and scribes were grumbling one day about Jesus. "This fellow welcomes sinners and eats with them" (Luke 15:2). From the perspective of the Pharisees and their scribes, Jesus associates with people who have lost their way, who have left the straight and narrow, who have left the fold, as it were. Not only does Jesus welcome them, he eats with them; he hangs out with them, which infuriates the religious leaders. Jesus probably prefers the company of honest sinners than self-righteous religious. And so what Jesus does is remarkable: instead of judging them for being sinners, instead of keeping them at arms' length, instead of being moralistic about it all, Jesus offers them a still more excellent way (cf. 1 Corinthians 12:31).

Jesus tells the Pharisees a parable: "Which of you, having a hundred sheep and losing one of them, does not leave the ninety-nine in the wilderness and go after the one that is lost until he finds it? When he has found it, he lays it on his shoulders and rejoices. And when he comes home, he calls together his friends and neighbors, saying ... 'Rejoice with me'" (Luke 15:4-6).

Many here have heard this parable before, of the shepherd who leaves the ninety-nine to go after the one lost sheep. We know *about* the story, but the text requires more than knowledge. It asks for something more: Are you *in* the story? Is this your story? Is it your experience? Can you feel what Jesus is saying here?

To help us get there it might be useful to compare Luke's version of the parable with Matthew's. In Luke 15, we have three parables, the lost sheep, lost coin, and the lost (prodigal) son.

Matthew's take is different. Turn to Matthew 18:12. The parable of the shepherd is given in the context of Jesus' teaching on how we care for our children. "If a shepherd has a hundred sheep, and one of them has gone astray, does he not leave the ninety-nine on the mountains and go in search of the one that went astray? And if he finds it, truly I tell you, he rejoices." Looks plain enough, doesn't it? Appears the same as Luke.

Now turn again to Luke 15:4. Does not the shepherd "leave the ninety-nine in the wilderness and go after the one that is lost until he finds it? When he has found it, he lays it on his shoulders and rejoices."

Did you hear it, do you see the subtle yet significant difference, the contrasting theological slant of Matthew and of Luke? In Matthew, the shepherd goes looking for the lost sheep, but it's uncertain whether or not he'll find it. "And *if* he finds it…" The outcome is in doubt. What does Luke say? The shepherd will go after the one that is lost *until* he finds it and he won't stop *until* he finds it. There's no question about the outcome because it says "when he has found it" he will place it on his shoulders, rejoicing all the way home. Luke adds, "And when he comes home, he calls together his friends and neighbors, saying to them, 'Rejoice with me, for I have found my sheep that was lost'" (Luke 15:6).

My sheep that was lost. My sheep that was lost. My sheep! Luke's version makes bold theological claims. From Luke's perspective, there's no question that the lost will be found. In fact, Jesus says that even when lost, the sheep still belong to him. Even when we're lost, we're not really lost because even when we stray, we still belong to the Lord. The psalmist knew this truth when he affirmed, "Where can I go from your spirit? Or where can I flee from your presence? If I ascend to heaven, you are there; if I make my bed in Sheol, you are there" (Psalm 139:7-8). But when we do get lost (and we do and we will), the good news is that the Lord never rests until we're found and brought back home.

You see, this is who God is; this is a profound *image* of God that Jesus is placing before us. This is who God is and this is what God does. Indeed, God never rests until all the lost have been brought home. The lost might not know it or even feel it—when you're lost, it feels like you're all alone—but the Lord of Love is searching for you. You might feel that you're not worthy of such love, that you're beyond hope, beyond help. You might feel that, but that's not the full story. The full story, the deeper, broader story is that you are worthy, worthy of God's hot pursuit to find you and bring you back, up on his shoulders, rejoicing all the way home. *There's no judgment for getting lost, only rejoicing over being found.* It's a joy that the shepherd is eager to share with his friends and neighbors: *Come and see who's back! Look who is here! Look who's home!* This is what Scripture means by grace. *Grace finds us when we're lost, lifts us up, and then takes us home rejoicing.* And this is what grace feels like.

The irony here, though, is that for us to know what grace feels like, *really* feels like, we first have to be lost or acknowledge that we are, already, lost. It's no mistake that Dante Alighieri (c. 1265-1321) begins the *Divine Comedy*, his story of descending into hell and ending before the beatific vision of God, with these words. The first lines of the *Inferno*, part one of the Comedy, are:

> In the midway of this our mortal life,
> I found me in a gloomy wood, astray
> Gone from the path direct… (*Inferno*, Canto 1).

He lost his way. And now the journey begins. The one's who have been to hell and back know what it means to be found. The prodigal had to leave home and fall, badly, hit rock bottom, even eat with the pigs, in order for him to discover who he was and discover how much his father really cared about him. We have to get lost in order to be found. This is what theologians call the happy fall," *felix culpa*.[1] Those who are never lost never know what it feels like to be found.

The history of the church is full of women and men who give witness to this truth. Look at John Newton (1725-1807), who wrote the hymn "Amazing Grace." He knew what a wretch he was as a slave trader. It's in the midst of his sin, his brokenness, his apparent alienation from God that he discovers God's transforming love. The same was true for the apostle Paul. Even though he was, as he admits, a "blasphemer, persecutor, and a man of violence," (1 Tim. 1:13), he still received mercy. "And the grace of our Lord overflowed for me," he said, "with the faith and love that are in Christ Jesus. The saying is sure and worthy of full acceptance"—in other words, Paul says, trust me, I know— "Christ Jesus came into the world to save sinners—of whom I am the foremost" (1 Tim 1:15).

I wish more people in the Church knew that they're not really lost, but are already found, that they ultimately belong to the Lord. As J.R.R. Tolkien (1892-1973) knew, "Not all who wander are lost." I wish more people in the world knew that they're not really lost, but already found, that they ultimately belong to the Lord. Always have. Always will. And that the Lord will not rest until he finds us, until we know that we've been found, until he gets to rejoice with us and over us.

But knowing about all of this is not enough. We need to feel it within, to see ourselves within the story. This might help, a guided imagery, a way into the story. I invite you to close your eyes. Relax.

Imagine that lost sheep wandering from the fold…
Look at that lost sheep…

---

[1] Cf. Aldo Carotenuto, *To Love, To Betray: Life as Betrayal* (Wilmette, IL: Chiron Publications, 1996), vii-viii, 145. G. W. F. Hegel (1770-1830) also referred to this as the "upward falling."

Imagine it found.
Imagine the weight of the sheep on Jesus' shoulders, being carried along…
Now, imagine that you're that lost sheep,
afraid, alone, cut off, anxious, worried…
See yourself found by the one who loves you and has been searching for you…
See yourself lifted up by the Shepherd, feel his strength underneath you, as he carries you on his shoulders, maybe the way your mother or father used to carry you as a girl or boy.
Imagine the Shepherd rejoicing because you've been found…
Now, see yourself arriving home,
hear the joy in the Shepherd's voice,
hear it with the ear of your heart,
"Look who've I've found. Look who's back. Rejoice with me…."

Home. Home, indeed.

A World of Distractions

Luke 10:38-42

When I sent out the worship preview for this Sunday, I included a chaotic looking diagram that attempts to map all the ways we try and fail to maintain focus in our lives.[1]

At the center is an image of a man touching his temples, as if to soothe a headache, with a caption that reads, "How to focus in the age of distraction." Around him are all the various ways we try to organize and focus our lives, only to discover that all these schemes become further distractions. We create rituals or habits around how we begin our day or how we end our day. We manage how and when we respond to email. We take the time to reflect and review the day and come up with ideas to make tomorrow even more efficient, even more productive. We have lists—and lists for lists. We schedule time for digital technology detox—no television, no Facebook, no email, smart phones. We try to enjoy more time with our family and friends. We organize all the paper in our home and office, get rid of clutter, make sure all the dishes are clean and empty the sink before we leave the house in the morning. We'll eat better. Sleep better. Make time for exercise. Make time

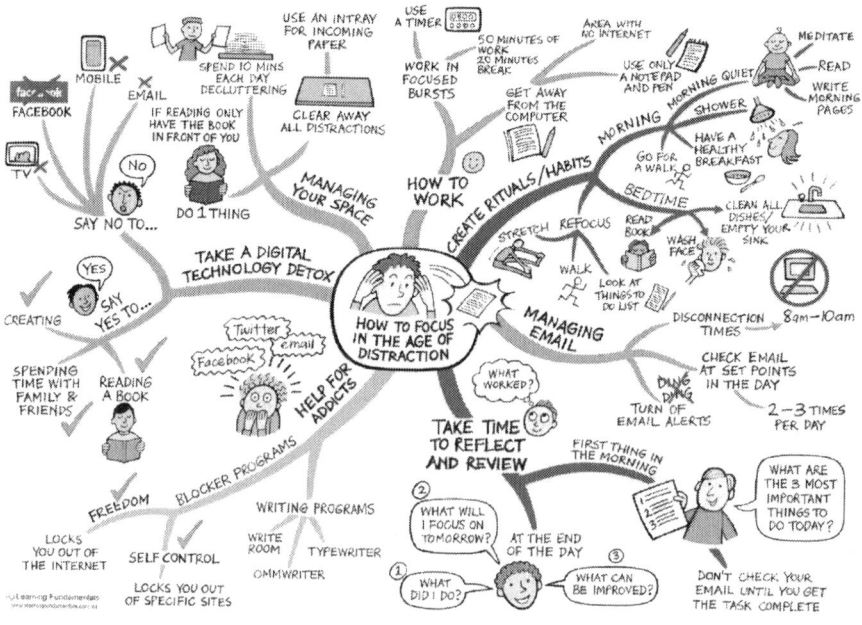

---

[1] http://learningfundamentals.com.au/presentations/focus/.

for prayer, for worship. We set up strategies to help us focus, but it seems the more we do these the more difficult it is to be focused.

Can you relate? Is this how you feel? Do have a headache just thinking about all of this? You're not alone.

How do we focus in this age of distraction? It's even more demanding for those who struggle with Attention Deficit Disorder. There's always someone or something vying for our attention, pulling us away from the things and people that matter most in our lives. We're running in ten thousand directions all at the same time. We're being pulled in so many different directions that it's difficult to focus. And when we ignore or neglect the things and people worthy of our time, the guilt and the shame set in. The guilt and shame are fueled by *anxiety*, which seems to be a steady hum underneath everything these days.

Jesus' visit to the home of Mary and Martha in Bethany could have happened yesterday. It has a contemporary feel to it, doesn't it? It's a remarkable visit, a remarkable conversation that occurs here in only four verses—four verses intentionally placed by Luke between the story of the lawyer who was anxious about inheriting eternal life, to which Jesus provided the radical Parable of the Good Samaritan (Luke 10:25-37), as we saw last week, followed by Jesus' teaching on prayer, showing us how to pray in the Lord's Prayer (Luke 11:1-13).

Mary and Martha are a study in contrasts. Martha welcomes Jesus into their home. She extends hospitality. She does what is expected of her. Mary takes a break from her work, sits at Jesus' feet, and listens to what he has to say. It's easy to pit them against each other. Martha represents the active life, the worker-bee, the go-getter. Mary represents the contemplative life, passive, lackadaisical, maybe a mystic. Jesus obviously favors Mary's way of being. But it's not simply either-or here. Both of these personality types have value. Although they are both women, these types have little to do with gender. There's a Martha and Mary in each of us.

That said, because of the way the text is constructed, it's the Martha-type that Jesus is most concerned about—*not* because it's wrong or sinful—but because Jesus knows the way Martha's moving through her life is hindering her from being attentive to what is right before her very eyes. She can't see because she's distracted. She can't focus her attention on God's visitation where she lives because, in a sense, she's not home, she's not there. She's someplace else in her head. She can't be in the moment. She's in the future, considering what has to be done. Therefore, she can't be attentive to what's moving right in front of her.

Why is Martha like this? It's clear that she resents Mary. So where does resentment come from? Resentment is often connected to jealousy. And jealousy is often a vector of desire, that is, it indicates what we really want for ourselves. Did Martha harbor a secret desire to be more like Mary? Perhaps knowing how difficult that would be for her, to be like Mary, Martha feels unappreciated for what she does contribute to the running of the household. When we feel unappreciated it seems like no one really understands us, no one cares about us. Her resentment toward Mary then spills over toward Jesus. "Lord, do *you* not care that my sister has left me to do all the work by myself?" Is she now lumping Mary and Jesus together here, implying that he, too, doesn't care? Is she suggesting that he, too, doesn't appreciate "all the work" she's doing?

"All the work by myself," Martha says. Well, that's what she says. But is she telling the truth? Is she really doing "all the work" by herself? It sounds like she's having a pity party. It sounds like exaggeration. If it is, then exaggeration is often a mask meant to cover over or hide something, that prevents others from seeing what's really going on there underneath. How much of "all the work" is really necessary work? How much is unnecessary?

It's clear that Martha likes to keep busy and she values being busy and expects others to be just like her—task oriented, driven, busy—and she's quick to judge others who don't measure up the same way. She's so bothered by this that she pulls Jesus into her frustration— *"you tell her."* This is a classic triangulation move, which is never healthy in interpersonal relations. Triangulation is when you ask someone to say or do something that you're unwilling to say or do yourself directly. Triangulation is never good.

On the other hand, Mary could just be lazy and Martha knows it. Maybe Mary has always been allergic to work. Maybe Mary has always been a dreamer and never had much of a drive. We don't know. Maybe she's bored by housework and chores and hungers for something more that Jesus now represents? We're not sure.

It's clear, though: Martha is the busy-bee in the house. An admirable quality, *to be sure!* But every quality, indeed every virtue, also has a shadow side. In our age we think the busy person is important. We might complain about being busy all the time, but some actually thrive on it. We want to be seen as busy, we don't want to be seen by anyone, especially our boss, as being inactive, doing nothing. The more we do, the busier we are, and the more important we think we are.

A lot of pastors fall into this trap. A friend calls this the Busy Pastor Syndrome. *How are you, pastor? How are things at the church?* "Oh, busy, very busy, crazy busy. So much is going on at the church. We're just crazy busy."

(Meaning, *I'm busy; therefore I'm important.*) But what does it really mean to be busy?

Sometimes, not all the time, but sometimes busyness is a compulsion, a compulsion that hides a mass of insecurities and fears. Writing last year in *The New York Times*, Tim Kreider suggests that "Busyness serves as a kind of existential reassurance, a hedge against emptiness; obviously your life cannot possibly be silly or trivial or meaningless if you are so busy, completely booked, in demand every hour of the day."[2]

A hedge against emptiness. Is that what our busyness really is? Is that why we're so distracted? We might complain about distractions, having difficulty focusing, but I wonder if at some unconscious level the opposite is really true: we want to be distracted, we don't want to be focused or attentive to what's before us. There's considerable anxiety under all of this, I know. For what if I don't like what I find, what if I don't like what I'm *feeling* when I stop, when I'm focused and aware? What if it's all empty, all hollow underneath? Who are we when we stop?

The Greek word used here for *distraction* means to be pulled or dragged away, drawn in different directions. When this happens it feels as if we're being determined by some power or force that is pulling us away from the center. It's like being in the sway or under the influence of an orbital force, a kind of gravitational pull, a force that overwhelms us and hinders our ability to pull away. Even if we want to pull away, we can't. We're trapped.

Psychologists have a word for this: *complex*. A complex is the concentration of energy around an emotionally-charged experience, memory, fear, or anxiety. A complex is made up of "psychic elements—ideas, opinions, convictions—that are grouped around emotionally sensitive areas."[3] All of this is going on in the unconscious. When we are in the thrall of a complex—and we all have them, many of them—we feel like we're in the grip of something. Actually, you don't have a complex; a complex has you. For example, we're going along in our day, something happens, someone says something, a changed mood sweeps over us. That's a complex. When a complex has us we might feel caught or trapped or hindered. We might say something that we really don't want to say, or do something out of character. You can hear it in the language we use, "Something came over me, and I don't know why I said that … or did that." Most significantly, *a complex often*

---

[2] Tim Kreider, "The 'Busy' Trap," *The New York Times*, June 30, 2012. http://opinionator.blogs.nytimes.com/2012/06/30/the-busy-trap.
[3] June Singer, *Boundaries of the Soul: The Practice of Jung's Psychology* (New York: Anchor Books, 1994), 43ff. Jungian analytic theory was originally known as complex psychology.

usurps our ability to choose or act in a way that we wish. As a result, a complex can hinder us from seeing and living in reality.

As I was reading the text again this week it felt like Martha was caught in a complex. We might call this the Martha Complex. It's clear that she's in a state—frustrated, resentful, feeling unappreciated, full of activity. But what's going on under the surface? What's stirring there? Why is Martha so anxious? What's hindering her from choosing wisely? This obviously wasn't an issue for Mary. Mary chose wisely. And what she has cannot be taken away from her (Lk 10:42). This means that Martha chose unwisely. Martha's caught up in her "stuff"; her "stuff" colors what she sees and informs her choices. As a result, she misses what's there before her; she misses the Holy in her midst.

And what does Jesus do? *"Martha, Martha"*—did he take her by the arms, I wonder, crossing her path, holding her shoulders, speaking directly into her eyes? *"Martha, Martha, stop. Look at me. Let me look at you"*—as if to break the spell of the complex, discharging its energy. *"Martha, Martha, you are worried and distracted by many things. This really isn't about all the work and the chores, is it? You are worried, concerned, anxious."* The Greek here suggests that her mind was agitated. *"You're freighted with care, Martha."*

"There is only one thing needed," Jesus said. When we're worried and distracted, we're pulled in ten thousand directions and pulled away from the one thing needed: *to dwell lovingly in the presence of God, to sit at Jesus' feet, to be attentive to him, to God, to the movement of the Spirit within our hearts.* Or to put it a different way, this is a life grounded and centered in God. This is what matters most. This is what our souls hunger for. When we are distracted and worried, we get pulled away from the One who holds us and sustains us.

We need more opportunities in our lives to just *stop*. Who are we when we remove the distractions? What's left? When we're not working—work, too, can be a distraction—who are we, who is left? Do you know who is left? *Who is left is the real self, the true you;* the authentic self that wants to dwell in the presence of God and it's this deeper, authentic self—the true you—that God desires to be in a relationship with, less the busy, compulsive, anxious self.

So what do we do with the distractions? We can try to come up with strategies to remove them. Or how about just taking the time to stop, to pray, simply be with God? To get to that place of being with God we need to embrace silence—we need much more silence in our lives. That's why contemplative practices and worship experiences such as Taizé, which incorporates fifteen minutes (or longer) of silence into the service, are so essential in our lives.

When we enter the silence, we come to know what Hinduism correctly calls "the monkey brain." It's our brains, our minds running in nonstop activity with no direction or purpose. When I was in India several weeks ago, I had monkeys living all around my cottage. They were out in the front yard, up in the trees, chasing each other over the roof of the cottage. They were frenetic and always nervous, hyper vigilant. In the silence we will meet our monkey brains; then we'll see just how distracted we really are.

It makes sense why the parable about loving one's neighbor as oneself and loving God are followed by Jesus' teaching on prayer. That should tell us something. Prayer, especially silent prayer, actually allows us to be more focused and less distracted. Silent prayer, dwelling in God, can actually help release us from some of our complexes. When we are silent before God, with silence focused, it's remarkable how less distracted we become, how more focused we become.

The bulletin reads "sermon" then "season of silence." But I want to make the silence part of the sermon by providing an opportunity to practice what I've been preaching: to be still, to dwell in God's presence. So let us enter into a season of silence. As a guide through this time, you might wish to read slowly to yourself Edwina Gateley's poem "Let Your God Love You." So let us be silent and be still:

> Be silent.
> Be still.
> Alone.
> Empty
> Before your God.
> Say nothing.
> Ask nothing.
> Be silent.
> Be still.
> Let your God look upon you.
> That is all.
> God knows.
> God understands.
> God loves you
> With an enormous love,
> And only wants
> To look upon you
> With that love.
> Quiet.
> Still.
> Be.
> Let your God—
> Love you. [4]

---

[4] Edwina Gateley's poems may be found here: edwinagateley.com.

The Call to Listen

Luke 9:28-36
Transfiguration of the Lord

This is one my favorite Sundays of the year. The transfiguration—whether it's Matthew's or Mark's or Luke's version—is one of my favorite stories in the New Testament. The fact that Matthew and Mark and Luke (the Synoptic Gospels) include this event tells us that it was pivotal in Jesus' life and significant because it reveals something essential about Jesus' identity and God's glory at work through him. It's not the only story shared by them. The feeding of the five thousand and the last supper, the crucifixion, and of course the resurrection are included by these three witnesses. (John's Gospel is a "horse of a different color," as it were, which is why I'm leaving him out.) But my point here is that while the Synoptic Gospels refer to the Transfiguration, placing it almost at the center of their narratives, letting it serve in some ways as the hinge upon which their narratives hang, for the most part, its importance has been ignored or overlooked. It's a text that leaves us feeling puzzled and confused. A lot of my friends and colleagues don't like to preach on this text. What do we do with a text like this?

I would probably feel the same way but for the fact that almost twenty-three years ago this September this text and its meaning took on enormous significance for me. At every ordination in the Presbyterian Church (USA), in addition to the sermon, there's a charge directed to the ordinand and a charge to the calling congregation. At my ordination, I asked a Princeton Seminary professor, mentor, and friend, James Loder, to give the charge. He walked into the pulpit of my home church, the First Presbyterian Church of North Arlington, NJ, just a few feet from the font at which I was baptized 26 years earlier, read this text (Matthew's version) and then proceeded to offer a second sermon on it.

I can still hear Jim's voice in my ears, saying to me, charging me to, "Listen to him. Listen to him." Jim said to me, a week before I left for Scotland, that the life, the vitality, the effectiveness of my ministry wherever I go, wherever I serve will always be contingent upon my capacity to "Listen to him." My failures and successes in ministry will be directly related to my ability to "Listen to him."

If that sounds heavy, it is. That's what a calling is, it's a burden, a weight we've been asked to carry. That's what these stoles represent, the yoke of the calling, being yoked to Christ. When I arrived at St. Leonard's Parish Church in St.

Andrews, Scotland, where I served, I was struck by the large stained-glass west window in the sanctuary with a depiction of Jesus' transfiguration. Since then, transfiguration features prominently in my journey and has shaped my faith and theological outlook.

Jim's words are never far from me. Over these twenty-three years as a minister I have tried to listen, worked hard at listening. Sometimes faithful, I like to think; but also, I know, at times faithless. Jim was right. Listening matters. Listening to Christ is what counts. Listening has changed my life for the good and hopefully for others who listen to me.

But it's only now, twenty-three years later, that I'm beginning to sense something else about this text; I'm beginning to sense how much I've heard "Listen to him" primarily as a command, instead of hearing it as something else—and it's the something else that I'll get to in a minute.

Until recently, my own *moralizing ear* was getting in the way of me hearing the text. The *moralizing ear* so often distorts our capacity to hear and perceive grace in scripture. *Moralizing ear* is my term for a filter that often informs our hearing of scripture. (Those in the Thursday Morning Bible Study have heard me talk about this over the years.) What I mean here is that somehow, some way, so many have come to assume that faith is primarily about following the rules, about laws, proper behavior, commandments, and, of course, judgment if we fail to obey. With such a perspective, God is essentially seen as a lawgiver. Many hold the view: God created human beings to behave, we screwed up, so we're judged, forced to pay the price—a price we cannot afford to pay because who is "rich" enough in virtue to make up for Adam's fall, so Jesus comes along, pays the price instead, and, even though we're now forgiven, with his help we can follow the law, because God only cares about whether or not we follow the law.

Such a view, which I've intentionally made to sound simplistic and foolish (which I think it is), is produced by the moralizing part of us, ruled by an image of God as Lawgiver. When we do this we reduce the *function* of religious faith to morals, to ethics; it's called moralizing. This tendency is old and deep and it's all over the church and it shapes external views of Christianity. During the Enlightenment, when Reason tried to reign and anything mystical or supernatural was deemed "unreasonable," philosophers such as Immanuel Kant (1724-1804) said most of Christianity should be rejected because it wasn't rational. The only rational purpose religion served was to teach and reinforce morality. Religion was purely functional.[1] Religion serves society by making us moral, making sure that we all behave. Kant reduced religion to

---

[1] For example, see Kant's *Religion within the Limits of Reason Alone* (1793), among other works.

ethics and helped to turn faith into an ethical code, a law, and in many ways the Church is still suffering from his error. I consider this to be an extremely serious issue because it hinders us from really hearing the gospel. (One day, when I find the time, I want to write a book on this.)

Yes, ethics, morals matter. Of course they do. Rules matter. How we behave matters. But to suggest that *this* is the good news of the Christian gospel, that Jesus died on the cross to appease an angry Judge-Father and now expects you to behave because any moment he's going to lash out at you in anger, to suggest that you're only loved if you behave in a certain way, is a gross misrepresentation and misunderstanding of the height and depth and reach of God's grace! It cheapens the gospel.

This brings us back to the text. Words such as "Listen to him" can easily be heard as one more command, one more rule, one more thing to do, one more standard to try to live up to. Heard through the filter of the moralizing ear, that's what we think it means and so we get to work and soon we're judging ourselves for our behavior, whether we're listening or not listening.

But, no one listens all the time, right? Right? No one listens all the time. You might hear someone talking, but that doesn't mean you're really listening.

Now, of course, "Listen to him" is a command. There's no way around this. It's an imperative. *But who is offering the command?* Whose voice is speaking from the cloud that engulfs Peter, James, and John? Luke says, "Then from the cloud came a voice that said, 'This is my son, my Chosen; listen to him!'" Other early versions of Luke's Gospel read, "This is my son, my Beloved; listen to him!" It's this latter reading that echoes the divine voice that we heard coming from the heavens as Jesus came up out of the waters of his baptism, "This is my son, my Beloved, in whom I am well pleased" (Luke 3:22). The Voice speaking to the disciples *refers to* the object of his love, the *Beloved.* If Jesus hears these words as the Beloved, if love is being directed toward him, then the source of the Voice must know something about love; for the Voice is love itself. So, yes, we hear a command, but it's voiced in love, by the one who *is* love. Yes, it's a command. But when we remember that the Voice is love, then the command is something else—and this is the something else that I didn't hear in Loder's charge to me 23 years ago—the command heard in love becomes something more. *It's really an invitation, an invitation to enter into the mystery and glory and love of God!*

To listen to him is to listen *in*, to listen in on God's deep conversation with humanity since the beginning of time; to listen to him is to listen *in* on God's deep desire for the world and our lives within it. When we listen to him we are included in that conversation. When we listen to him we are brought into a knowledge of God's deep desire for mercy and justice, for wholeness and healing, for love.² The command becomes an invitation: you and I are now welcomed to share—*share! share!*—in the very life of God, brought into the presence of God to receive a glimpse of God's glory and radiance shining through Jesus. We are drawn, like Moses and Elijah, into a deep relationship with the Source of all being and goodness and light and given insights and wisdom and knowledge that we could never obtain on our own, things reason cannot handle or fathom, experiences that are new and therefore disorienting and thereby reorienting.

Peter, James, and John are terrified by this revelation; they talk nonsense because their frame of reference and meaning could not comprehend what they were experiencing. Instead, their reality was being reframed by a larger reality, as they came to see the story of their lives as participating in a much larger story of divine salvation that reached back to Moses and forward toward what was about to happen on a cross in Jerusalem and beyond, even to a future held by the light of glory. They are commanded to listen to him and thus invited into the very life shared between Jesus and God. This is relational language. When we listen to someone we are pulled into that person's life; when we're listening to Christ we're pulled into that relationship, the divine-human relationship, and that is what matters above all else. *When that happens reality is reframed and reality reframed is what it means to be transfigured.³ That's what Love does, it transfigures our lives.* This *is what the gospel is all about.* This *is good news with power that shakes the foundations of the world and reorients our lives.*

The Voice that spoke from the cloud continues to speak to us; it continues to summon us to listen. In the church we often use listening language when we're trying to discern God's call in our lives. Many have difficulty discerning God's call or vocation in their lives. But maybe turning the phrase around might help us here; *what if first we are simply called to listen?* Listen to the Voice of Love speak and then discern your vocation. Listen to the Voice and then figure out how to act, what to do. Augustine (354-430) once said, "Love and do what you want." Vocation, then, doesn't come by trying to figure out what we're supposed to do with our lives; vocation comes from listening to the One who has given us life. One of the wisest voices of our time, Parker J. Palmer, writes, "Vocation does not come from willfulness. It comes from

---

² Here I hold to C. G. Jung's idea that our goal is not goodness, but wholeness. See also James Hollis, *Why Good People Do Bad Things: Understanding Our Darker Selves* (New York: Gotham Books, 2008), 234-235. The biblical scholar Marcus J. Borg makes a similar point, "Christian life is ultimately not about believing or about being good. Rather, it is about a relationship with God that involves us in a journey of transformation." *Meeting Jesus Again for the First Time: The Historical Jesus and the Heart of Contemporary Faith* (HarperOne, 1995), 2-3.
³ For a discussion on Loder and transfiguration, see Kenneth E. Kovacs, *The Relational Theology of James E. Loder: Encounter and Conviction* (New York: Peter Lang, 2011), 192, 194-196.

listening." The word *vocation* itself is rooted in the Latin for *voice*. "Vocation," Palmer writes, "does not mean a goal that I pursue. It means a calling that I hear. Before I can tell my life what I want to do with it, I must listen."[4]

If our first calling is to listen, then how do we do that? It's been said that listening is a skill, something we cultivate. Listening is a skill, and like all skills the more we practice them the better we are at using them. We can train ourselves to have better listening skills. Listening is an art, particularly the art of listening for what's being said and what isn't being said, listening for what's behind the words of a conversation. It's not surprising that truly listening is in short supply these days. It requires time. Listening is hard work. It can be exhausting. It also requires considerable energy and love and even courage.

Why courage? Because at least two other things are required: *silence* and *surrender*. Luke says, "When the voice had spoken, Jesus was found alone. And they kept silent" (Luke 9:36). In order to really listen, it's important for us to be *silent*. How can you listen if you're talking? The talking can be the audible kind done with our mouths or the ongoing internal chatter that fills our inner brains that never seems to quit. It's tough to listen to someone when there are competing conversations going on in our heads. Cultivating silence has always been a spiritual discipline, essential to the life of faith. This requires courage because we might not be happy with what we discover in the silence. What's true for human relationships is true for divine-human relationships. Interior silence is required; how else are you going to hear the still small voice of Love?

To listen also requires a kind of *surrendering*. Listening means you're open to what the other is saying; you have relinquished your control of what is said; you give up your privileged position and yield to what the other has to say. Instead of hearing what you want to hear or what you think someone is saying, you really listen. This, too, requires a form of courage. We might not like what we're hearing or we might disagree with it.

But more than anything else, especially when we're hearing the voice of Love, when we open ourselves and surrender to the other, we just might be changed and our reality transfigured. This is why men and women, each for their own reasons, have problems with surrendering because we hear this from the viewpoint of the ego, which equates surrender as weakness or defeat (particularly in men) or as submission to power, leaving one exposed to exploitation or abuse (particularly in women). We have to be careful here with surrender language, but if we don't use it we miss out on the gospel and

---

[4] Parker J. Palmer, *Let Your Life Speak: Listening for the Voice of Vocation* (Jossey-Bass, 2000), 4-5.

what Christians for centuries have told us, that, "surrender is an indispensable gateway to life, genuine freedom, and deep humanity."[5]

Without surrendering to the one who is Love, how can words such as these be heard as good news? "If any want to become my followers, let them deny themselves and take up their cross daily and follow me. For those who want to save their life will lose it, and those who lose their life—surrender their life—for my sake they will save it" (Luke 8:23-24). These words come in Luke just prior to his account of the Transfiguration.

When we listen to him, it means we are not listening to our egos or what others expect from us or the cacophony of voices in our heads or on television or the crowd; we are yielding, surrendering to him, surrendering to Love.

Silence and surrender. Two good disciplines for disciples to follow through Lent and beyond. In these forty days of Lent may we have the courage to welcome more silence, both within and without, and listen to him more profoundly, surrendering our lives into his arms, arms that will carry us where we need to go. We are invited by Love to listen, to listen to him who is love, and in our love for him, we listen.

---

[5] David G. Benner, *Soulful Spirituality: Becoming Fully Alive and Deeply Human* (Brazos, 2011), 157. I'm grateful for Dr. Benner's entire discussion of the centrality of surrender in the Christian life (156-168).

A Wild, Wondrous Journey

Matthew 4:1-11
First Sunday in Lent

Temptation seems to fill the air during Lent; Lent seems to be organized around it. The lectionary for this first Sunday in Lent begins with Jesus tempted by the devil in the wilderness. It casts its shadow over these forty days. Temptation is the enemy that requires our vigilance and diligence, especially if you felt called to give up something for Lent: chocolate, alcohol, television, Facebook. Can you free yourself from the Tempter's power? Can you make it all the way to Holy Week?

There's no way around it. Temptation is all over this text. Three times the devil tries to unnerve Jesus and obstruct him from his mission. After forty days Jesus is famished, exhausted, weak, tired, thirsty, hungry. And then the Tempter arrives.

This really is a remarkable text. It's easy to be drawn into it, dropped down into this dramatic setting, this place of struggle and anguish. This is a vivid story made for cinema or television.

It's also a problematic text in that it's easy to come away with all kinds of views regarding the devil and temptation, some of which are not helpful. I've met Christians who live in a perpetual state of fear and anxiety that they might not be strong enough to sustain a full court press from the Tempter. They think the devil is under every stone, around every corner, just waiting for an opportune time to tempt and attack, deceive and destroy Christians. There's a kind of paranoia that sets in as they wait for the devil to trick them. They're always on guard. This is not a healthy way to live; neither is it a joyful way to live.

The temptation is real in this story—and it's serious. These are not trivial amusements trying to lull Jesus away from his work. He's being tempted by desire, materialism, tempted by power, tempted by influence and glory, tempted by *religion*. He's being tempted with an alternative narrative for his life, "If you are the Son of God ..." *If.* Does Jesus know that he's the Son of God? Is this what he's really wrestling with in the wilderness? And if he consents, if he claims this identity, accepts this power, what then? How does one then *live* with such an identity, how does one make use of such power?

That's really what's at stake here. Yes, it's about temptation. But it's about more than temptation. To focus on temptation is a moralistic reading of this text. It's more than simply a warning: watch out, the devil will tempt us, don't give into temptation. This would be a surface reading of the text.

We know there's more to it than this because of one word. It's one word that's often overlooked in the hearing of this story. And that one word is *Spirit* (Matthew 4:1).

After Jesus' baptism, the Spirit of God *sends* Jesus into the wilderness to be tempted. His temptation is ordered, directed, not by the devil, as it were, but by the Spirit of God. The devil is not doing anything here beyond the purview of God's providence. The Spirit *sends* Jesus into the wilderness to be tempted. And if the Spirit is God's Spirit and if God's Spirit is love, then we have to conclude that it's for the sake of love, the Spirit's love for Jesus that he's sent deep into the wilderness of Judea. Then we could say that it's love that sends him into this space. This might sound odd and strange and not very loving. But it's for the sake of God's love for him and, I would argue, God's love for *us* that he's sent into the wilderness. Why? Because there were things Jesus needed to discover about himself that could only be discovered in the wilderness. There were things he needed to struggle with that could only be experienced there in the wilderness. There were things he could only discover in the struggle, in the fight, in the wrestling.

There are things *we* can only discover about ourselves when we, too, have been thrown into the wilderness. There are things that we only begin to really, honestly, struggle with when we are thrown into wild, unfamiliar places. There are things we discover about ourselves and our neighbors, the world, even God, when we are in the fight, when we're struggling to survive, when we're lost in the search for meaning, when we're wrestling with our demons, putting them in their place, and then coming out on the other side of it all with the angels of God waiting on us and tending to us (Matthew 4:11).

I don't know why it has to be this way. But it is. I don't know why the world is ordered this way. But it is. This seems like a risky, even precarious way for God to order human life. Why can't we just discover these things without the struggle and the fight and the wrestling? I don't know.

But there are at least two things I do know. First, what I do know and what this text seems to suggest is that a wilderness is required—an unfamiliar territory of some kind. It could be a geographic place, a life-situation or experience, or, psychologically, the vast terrains of the human heart. We can stay home, remain forever in the familiar, but then we'll miss out on discovering what the soul truly hungers for.

The hard truth is that "Great issues affecting [humankind] always have to be decided in the wilderness." These are the words of Alfred Delp (1907-1945), written in Tegel Prison, Berlin, Epiphany 1945, where Dietrich Bonhoeffer (1906-1945) was also a prisoner for a time. Delp was a Jesuit priest, theologian, philosopher, who was part of an assassination attempt against Adolf Hitler (1889-1945). "Great issues affecting [humankind] always have to be decided in the wilderness; in uninterrupted isolation and unbroken silence. They hold a meaning and blessing these great, silent, empty spaces that bring [one] face to face with reality."[1] These are extraordinary words written in the wilderness of a prison cell.

The second thing is this. What I do know and what this text seems to suggest is that, like Jesus, we need to be pushed up against our limits. Our limitations must be exposed. It's not unlike what an athlete in training experiences. Places such as deserts and wildernesses are good at doing this for us—places known for their silence, their emptiness, places untamed, places that don't care about us, don't care whether or not we survive, that are completely indifferent to our wants and needs. Life situations can bring us to our limits. When we come up against our mortality—the ever ashen-quality of our lives—that we are dust, this is also a limiting thought.

Now all of this can be depressing, I know. That's what you're probably thinking. This doesn't have to be, but it often is. These are not essentially happy thoughts. But don't blame me. It's part of the Christian message but perhaps not the best evangelism tool. Churches don't generally grow with this kind of message. You don't find it on church signs: **Join us at 10:30 a.m. and discover your limitations! Refreshments will be served.**

And, yet, this is the difficult, demanding, heart-breaking, achingly beautiful and gracious message of the gospel: *there is liberation and release when we discover our limits.* This is what T. S. Eliot (1888-1965) was getting at in his poem "Little Gidding," one of the poems in *Four Quartets*. Little Gidding is a small village in England, with an old Anglican Church and cemetery, which Eliot visited in 1936. In this poem he's talking about the poet's use of language as a metaphor for the Christian life.

> Every phrase and every sentence
> is an end and a beginning,
> Every poem is an epitaph—epitaph, as on a gravestone.
>
> Any action is a step to the block, to the fire,
> down the sea's throat
> Or to an illegible stone: and that is where we start.

---

[1] Alfred Delp, "Epiphany 1945: The Law of the Wilderness." http://pedrokolbe.wordpress.com/2014/01/08/epiphany-1945-the-law-of-the-wilderness.

The illegible stone is an old tombstone, with the name worn away by the elements, by time. *That* is where we start. That is where the Christian life begins, that's where the journey begins. Eliot is drawing here upon the wisdom of the English mystic Julian of Norwich (1342-c.1413) who said, "In my end is my beginning."

The Spirit sends Jesus out into the wilderness to discover his limitations, to bring him up against his limits, in order for him to discover who he is and what he's capable of accomplishing. And he discovers this in the struggle with the Tempter. The Tempter doesn't have horns, a red suit, and a pitchfork. The devil, *diabolos*, in the Greek, means "one who throws things about." *(Dia* meaning through, around; *bolos*, meaning to throw.) The *diabolos* stirs things up, tries to confuse us, muddies the water, and distorts reality. He pushes Jesus. Tries to disorient him, confuse him, distort his reality, maybe even speak to his weaknesses and doubts and fears. And each time, Jesus pushes back, reaffirms what's true, and stays grounded.

In the face of these distractions, Jesus remains focused and committed to God's vision for his life. With each "attack" he reaffirms who he is and who he isn't. He comes to terms with his identity and his calling, all of it forged in the heat of the desert under the protective eyes of the Spirit. Now all of this was necessary in order to equip him for what was to come, to enable him to claim his identity, so that he could be faithful to the burden of the call placed upon his life. He then drew upon this experience throughout his ministry, especially in a garden, in the middle of the night, sweating blood, wrestling again with the purpose and meaning of his life (Luke 22:44).

The psychiatrist Carl Jung said, "Man needs difficulties, they are necessary for health."[2] Writing to clergy in 1932, Jung said, "Every psychic advance arises from the suffering of the soul."[3] This is *not* a glorification of suffering; neither is he saying that God causes suffering. But what Jung is trying to get at here, and I think he's right and worth our consideration, is that through our struggles, our desire to suffer through what we're confronted with, to undergo and struggle and resist and fight everything that is being thrown being at us from every direction to struggle, resist and fight, as Jesus did, we will discover something that we need to know. And not only what we need to know, as if this were merely an intellectual game, but something more,

---

[2] C. G. Jung, "The Transcendent Function," *The Collected Works of C. G. Jung*, Vol. 8 (Princeton: Princeton University Press, 1970), §143. Jung adds, "What concerns us...is only an excessive amount of them."
[3] C. G. Jung, "Psychotherapists or the Clergy," *The Collected Works of C. G. Jung*, Vol. 11 (Princeton: Princeton University Press, 1975) §497. Jung wrote, "...all creativeness in the realm of the spirit as well as every psychic advance of man arises from the suffering of the soul, and the cause of the suffering is spiritual stagnation, or psychic sterility."

something will be gained in our hearts, in our lives as Christians, an advance made, progress, development, growth in the Christian life, personal transformation, which has the potential to transform the world. And that's the good news here.

And there's one more sign of good news here. The number 40. It might be the Bible's way of saying "a very long time," but it's never empty time, it's never unending. It's actually a time of cultivation and growth, a time of preparation for what comes next. Every experience of 40—whether days or years—in scripture, whether it's Israel wandering for forty years in the wilderness of Sinai or Jesus in the wilderness of Judea—yields something new. Here we can see an *advance*, something gained from the experience. Jesus comes bursting out of this experience overflowing with spiritual energy, teeming with vitality, engaged, active, ready to take on the world, ready to preach the good news of God's Kingdom with passion, with strength, with compassion, with love.[4]

Altogether, Jesus shows us: this is what is means to be human, women and men in relationship with God. Jesus' way is our way, our way through Lent and beyond. His way is our way; our way is his way. This is the wild, wondrous journey we've been invited to share. So may we too pray, boldly, courageously: *Come, Holy Spirit, come.*

---

[4] Clarence Jordan, *The Substance of Faith: and Other Cotton Patch Sermons* (Wipf & Stock, 2013), 9ff.

Making All Things New
Revelation 21:1-8

This glorious text from Revelation 21 is often read at funerals or memorial services. There's so much about it that lends itself to such occasions in the life of the church. In a time of sorrow and grief these words offer considerable comfort: "See, the home of God is among mortals. He will dwell with them as their God; and they will be his peoples, and God himself will be with them; he will wipe every tear from their eyes. Death will be no more; mourning and crying and pain will be no more, for the first things have passed away" (Rev. 21: 3-4). Because of this reference to the death of death, of a time when mourning and crying and pain will come to an end, it is often assumed that this is a vision of the heavenly realm. Hence its use at funerals and memorial services. We suspect that these verses are describing a place in another world.

But the text doesn't say this. At the beginning of the chapter it reads, "Then I saw a new heaven and a new earth: for the first heaven and the first earth had passed away, and the sea was no more." It continues, "And I saw the holy city, the new Jerusalem, coming down out of heaven from God, prepared as a bride adorned for her husband." A new heaven and a new earth and in the earth a new city, a new Jerusalem. Where is it? Here in this world.

That's what John saw in his vision. (Revelation is an account of what he saw.) Now, we could say this was "just" a vision, a religious hallucination, a spiritual insight that has no real correspondence to reality as it is. Surely this can't be a description of *this* world because how on earth can there be on earth an earth without the sea—what kind of world would that be? Not a world we would want. That is unless you were a Jew. For a Jew such a world, without the sea, would be a kind of heaven because to the Jew the sea represented chaos, the part of creation that was beyond the control of God's sovereignty. Heaven would mean no sea. The Jews have never had a strong association with seas and oceans. You never think of Israel, for example, and say: naval power.

And, what is more, how can there really be a world where death is no more? Death from a purely biological perspective is a natural process of creation. No thing, no one lasts forever. Death is as sure as taxes, we say. But for a Jew, in Jesus' time, in most of the Bible, death meant more than biological death. Death was understood as a power, a force in the creation that is destructive, that hinders God's plans for creation. Paul refers to death as an enemy whose sting has been blunted by Jesus' resurrection from the dead (1

Corinthians 15:55-57). You can see why we assume that John's vision is of heaven: heaven as another world, some other dimension, some place other than here. The promises, the hope extended to God's people, we think, will be fulfilled and realized not in this world, but in a world to come.

But that's not what the text says. The text says heaven is a reality that comes down to earth, so that it "may be *on* earth," as we say in the Lord's Prayer, "as it is in heaven" (Matthew 5:10). The vision points to a place—a city. The Bible might begin in a garden, but it ends in a city. It's the city that matters to God. It's an urban setting where God chooses to pitch a tent to dwell with us and live with us, day in and day out. The city becomes the place where heaven and earth touch, meet—which is what the Jews believed about old Jerusalem, the *axis mundi*, the axis of the world, the center, the navel of the world. John's hopeful vision is not a description of a place beyond time, but a place in time, here and now.

This vision is really quite extraordinary, given the fact that John and his fellow Christians have been living through hell at the hands of the Romans. The fantastical, even violent, bloody images one finds in Revelation paint a picture of a world where Christians were seriously tortured and brutalized for their confession of Jesus as Lord instead of Caesar as Lord. One would expect that good news for these people—who have been victimized, broken, and abused by Rome—would be the promise of a new world someplace else. One would expect the promise of an afterlife in some other place would be their message. But, no; that's not what the text says. It's not the promise of some other world but this world that John sees. Revelation is not escapist, it's not otherworldly and there's no account of a rapture (or the whisking away of Christians at the so-called end of the world).[1]

Instead, listen to the voice of the one who sits on the throne, whose orb and scepter rule the universe with justice and righteousness, who rules even over the chaos of the sea, whose power of love cannot be matched by the force of death or the strength of Caesar's armies. Listen to what the voice on the throne says to John: "*See—behold—look—I am making all things new.*" Write these words: "It is done! I am the Alpha and the Omega, the beginning and end." The one who was there before time is the same faithful Lord at the end of time; the potentate of time who rules with love over the movement of our lives, the benevolent ruler who leads and moves all of creation towards its culmination and fulfillment, this is the one who says, "I am making all things new."

---

[1] Brian Blount, *Revelation* (Louisville: Westminster John Knox Press, 2009), 2.

With these amazing words at the end of Revelation, we are given a glimpse of the purpose and direction toward which God is moving the universe. They point to the culminating work of Jesus Christ, what his life and death and resurrection, his defeat of death all point to at the heart of existence. They give expression to the direction of all God's handiwork, the very purpose, goal, or end of the universe—which is the recreation and restoration of all things, the recreation and restoration of the world and our lives within it. This, my friends, is the force, the secret power deep at work in the depth of all things.

Now the text doesn't say the removal of all things. It doesn't say everything old will come to an end followed by something new. It doesn't say all new things. Instead, it says, "all things new."[2] This is what God loves to do, over and over and again, creating and recreating with all the "stuff" of our lives. Isaiah foreshadowed this when we hear God say, "I am about to do a new thing" (Isaiah 43:19). Or, here: "For I am about to create new heavens and a new earth" (Isaiah 65:17, see also 66:22).

God loves to take what is old or worn or broken or useless or tired and transform it. God loves to take into Godself all the hate, all the sin, all the excruciating pain and mind-numbing, heart-freezing sorrow of human existence and then do something marvelous and wonderful with it, offering something new in its place. God loves to take all of our tears and our hurts and our regrets, our shame and our guilt and then do something extraordinary with them, transforming them. God takes on every death force in ourselves, in our families and relationships, our communities, nations, and world and decisively redeems and restores. That's the goal, that's the purpose, that's what God is doing now and that's the direction of God's time. It's the promise of the Christian experience.

About eleven years ago, about a year before she died, I remember visiting my grandmother in the nursing home in New Jersey. My maternal grandmother lived with my family. Some of my earliest memories are with her. I couldn't say the word "grandma" as a toddler, so I said *Mama*. And that's who she was to me. I was extremely close to her. She was about 92 at the time, in declining health and suffering from dementia. It was a difficult visit. It was tough finding something to talk about, and she kept falling asleep. Although I had visited her there many times before, I couldn't help but remember the way she used to be: loving conversation, engaging me, asking questions. Frustrated, sad, and with nothing to talk about, after a few moments of silence, I said, "So, Mama, what else is new?" As I heard those words coming out of my mouth I thought to myself, how absolutely stupid you are—what

---

[2] Citing Eugene M. Boring's study *Revelation*, in Blount, 376.

was new for her when every day was relentlessly the same, where she was surrounded by death and the ravishment of time? All my pastoral care training, in that moment—gone. I asked it as if she wasn't even there. I felt terrible. Then she came to and turned to me and said, "Oh, Kenny, everything is new." And I smiled. *That* is the deeper truth of the universe because that's the deeper truth of the gospel.

The good news is that Jesus Christ declares to our hearts and to the heart of his church and to the heart of his world: "I am making all things new." At the core of the gospel is this experience of new life. At the core of our encounter with God is the same message: "Behold—*see!*—I make all things new."

Is it any wonder, therefore, that these words are among those used to describe the Christian experience: renewal, regeneration, rebirth, restoration, revitalization, redemption, change, new Creation? Transfiguration. Transformation. Conversion. Revolution. Resurrection? They all point to the same reality: the movement, the dynamism at the heart of the Christian life. There's nothing about it that calls us to secure the status quo. In fact, the status quo can too easily become *status woe*.

Woe, because there is something else within us, in our psyches, in the depths of our being that really doesn't like all of these words, that resists renewal or restoration or change. There's something in us that really doesn't embrace resurrection in our lives because that means something first must die in us. Until we come to terms with this resistance within us, until we face, head-on, our fear of rebirth, we will remain stuck. To acknowledge that Jesus is at work in our lives and the world, actually working to form and reform us, to give a place to the movement of God's Spirit blowing through our lives, can be very scary indeed. We prefer to keep God at bay. We prefer to think we're in control of our lives. We prefer to think we understand what it means to be a Christian and what God expects from us. There's no need for change.

"There's an old Celtic story," Parker Palmer writes, "about a monk who died and was interred in the monastery wall. Three days later, the monks heard noises coming from inside the crypt. When they removed the stone they found their brother alive. He was full of wonderment, saying, 'Oh, brothers, I've been there! I've seen it! And it's nothing at all like the way our theology says it is.' So they put him back in the wall and sealed the crypt again."[3]

It's an illusion to think we can wall-up the truth. It's an illusion to think we can resist forever the grace that seeks to enter into and work through our

---

[3] Told by Parker J. Palmer in "Taking Pen in Hand," *The Christian Century* (September 2, 2010), 25.

lives. It's an illusion to think that nothing will ever change, that we are bound by our circumstances or contexts or histories or our limited visions or even our budgets, and that there's nothing new under the sun. It's an illusion to think there's no cause for hope.

These illusions are really lies, because nothing can resist God's redemptive determination to restore, to heal, to make new. John tells his fellow Christians, yes, you've been through hell, but I've seen into the future and the future cannot compare to what is coming and has even now broken into our world. Because the future is in God's hands, this means the present is as well.

I invite you to meditate on Revelation 21:5, "Behold, I am making all things new," this week and claim this vision for yourself. Ask yourself: what this verse means in this season of your life. What does this verse say to your family situation? How does this inform your worship life and experience God's presence in the life of this community? What's in need of renewal in life? Where is God trying to regenerate new life in you? What is God through Christ trying to give birth in your or through you—and in us together—for the sake of the world?

As theologian Christopher Morse writes in his recent book on heaven, "We are called to be *on* hand for that which is *at* hand, but not *in* hand, an unprecedented glory of not being left orphaned but of being loved in a community of new creation beyond all that we can ask or imagine."[4]

To everything in the world that is worn and tired comes this word of good news, *"See, I am making all things new."*

To everyone who is weighed-down and weary and wants to begin again come these words of healing, *"See, I am making all things new."*

To every relationship, family, community, or church that hungers for a different way to be faithful and loving and forgiving come these words, *"See, I am making all things new."*

To everyone who wants rebirth and renewal come these words: listen to the one seated on the throne: *"See, I am making all things new." Alleluia. Alleluia!* Amen!

---

[4] Christopher Morse, *The Difference That Heaven Makes: Rehearing the Gospel* (London: T & T Clark, 2010), 122.

Weighed Down with Worry

Luke 12:22-31 (12:13-21)

"Therefore I tell you, do not worry ..."

About your life. About food. About clothes. Do not worry, Jesus says.

You're probably saying to yourself: *Easier said than done.* You're also probably reluctant to admit this, but my guess is you're thinking it. And then comes the guilt, because you know you worry, worry too much, and now you're feeling judged by Jesus. That never feels good.

But come on, Jesus. Really? Don't worry? Are you really human? Don't you know what it's like for us? Don't you know how complicated and scary the world can be? How is this even possible? Don't you know that we worry all the time and there's always one more person, one more news story, one more experience that tells us there's still more to worry about, that we ought to be worried? Don't you know that we worry—we're told we're supposed to worry—about our safety, about security. We worry about our health, worry about losing our health, worry about test results. We worry about money, not having enough, of never having enough. We worry about our family, our loved ones, our friends; we worry about our enemies and our foes. We worry about work, about finding a job, starting a new job, keeping a job. We worry about our problems, both small and big ones, the pressures that weigh us down and give us headaches and keep us awake at 3 a.m. We worry about threats and potential threats; we worry about tomorrow, about the future; we worry about climate change. We worry about all the things we hear on the news, and we worry about when the next natural disaster will strike, the next shooting, the next outbreak of war and violence. Don't you know that we worry all the time, Jesus?

And we worry about the meaning of our lives, whether or not our lives have purpose and direction. We worry about our faith, whether we have any left or just enough to be in your good graces. We worry about your church, what it will look like. Will we recognize it years from now, will it survive, will our children have faith? Sometimes we wonder if you're really there, if you really understand what it's like to be human: fallen, broken, frightened human beings in an enormously vast cosmos? Not to worry? And speaking of the cosmos, one day the sun is going to burn itself out. What then? What then?

Worry fills our lives these days. It's all around us. There are even some who take a strange comfort in worrying. It's what they do. It's how they fill the time. It's a way to cover over the anxiety that is actually underneath the worry, things that are too painful to acknowledge. We know, rationally, that most of the things we worry about will never happen. You know that, right? They just won't. They're fictive imaginings of an anxious mind looking for control. In this sense, the things we worry about are irrational, subrational, but that doesn't mean they don't get the best of us. We might claim to be very rational creatures, but it's the irrational things that are often driving our lives and our choices. So what are we to do?

Bobby McFerrin came up with one antidote to worry. You probably remember his Billboard Hot 100 hit from 1988, the a cappella song, "Don't worry," he sang, "Be Happy," sung to a kind of a carefree, Jamaican island rhythm. It's a fun tune. You can't help but feel happy singing along. But what happens when the song ends? McFerrin is actually quoting the Indian mystic Meher Baba (1894-1969) who believed he was an avatar, God in human form. He often said, "Don't Worry, Be Happy" when he cabled his followers in the West.

The imperative "be happy" isn't an antidote for worry; in fact, it could make matters worse. It doesn't give us a reason for happiness. It's not grounded in anything. It doesn't take seriously what is being felt and experienced in the moment.

You might say that Jesus, too, is offering an imperative, a command. "Do not worry." And it is a command, a strong command. What's the difference? It has nothing to do with being happy. Happiness is not the antidote. Jesus suggests that something else has already been given to us; the antidote to worry is already here for us and it's also coming, at the same time. But is Jesus right? Can we trust him? You have to answer that yourself.

So what's Jesus saying here? Don't worry about your life, what you will eat, or about your body, what you will wear. First, this message is *not* directed at those who are struggling to survive, people without food, clothing, or shelter. This message is directed at people who already have food and clothing, but want more and are anxious about obtaining it. Life is more than food and the body more than clothing. When Jesus says do not worry about your life. And life here, *psyche*, can be translated "soul," "one's whole being," the totality of your intrapsychic life. He's talking about a disposition or attitude of *soul*, and the soul has no reason to worry.

How can he say that? Just open your eyes, he says. *Consider! See!*

At this point Jesus uses a rhetorical strategy that was prevalent in Judaism at this time, it's found all over the Bible actually. It's called *qal wahoner*, meaning from light to heavy or less to great.[1] It's used to make an argument. It's a debate strategy. If something is true at a lower level, then it has to be even truer at a greater level.

Consider the ravens, Jesus said, "they neither sow nor reap, they have neither storehouse nor barn, and yet God feeds them." Yay, Ravens! God is on the side of the ravens! Now, you might think: okay, God cares for the birds. That's nice. But—and folks in Baltimore probably don't want to hear this—what's often overlooked here is that within Judaism ravens were considered unclean animals. Leviticus is very clear: "These you shall regard as detestable among the birds. They shall not be eaten; they are an abomination: the eagle, the vulture, the osprey, the buzzard … every raven of every kind" (Lev. 11:13-15). (Sorry, Ravens fans. Just quoting scripture.) What does Jesus say here, though? This is the radical part. If God provides for those detestable, abominable ravens, Jesus says, "Of how much more value are you than the birds!" From lesser to greater.

Jesus continues. "And can any of you by worrying add a single hour to your span of life?" Of course not. Why worry about the things you have no control over? Worry is an ineffective means of improving or changing our lives. It's just not productive.

Consider the lilies. The birds do not worry about food. The flowers don't worry about being clothed with beauty because they are already beautiful. They neither toil nor spin. They are what they are without any striving. In Jesus' day and before, there was no greater wealth or beauty or glory imaginable than King Solomon's. Yet, the flowers of the field exceed Solomon's glory. If God clothes the grass of the field with flowers, countless wildflowers, "how much more will he clothe you?" From lesser to greater.

So stop striving for these things, Jesus says. Stop grasping for these things. Stop the constant worrying. "Therefore, I tell you, do not worry …"

Now, you might be wondering why Jesus says, "Therefore." It points us to look at what comes before, because the larger context of this text begins at verse 13, in which Jesus offers the Parable of the Rich Fool. Jesus is warning here against greed. Greed is about grasping. "Be on guard against all kinds of greed; for one's life does not consist in the abundance of possessions" (Luke 12:15). And so Jesus tells the story of the rich fool who didn't have a place large enough to store all of his *stuff*, so he tore down what he had to build larger barns to store more *stuff* and then trusted in his *stuff* to give him plenty

---

[1] The first of rabbi Hillel's (c.110 BC–10 AD) rules of exegesis.

of happiness in the future, assuming that all his *stuff* was safely hoarded and secure. "But God said to him, 'You fool! This very night your life is demanded of you. And the things you have prepared, whose will they be?' So it is with those who store up treasures for themselves but are not rich toward God" (Luke 12:20-21).

This, then, is the context for Jesus' teaching on worry. The word for *worry* here means to be lifted up and raised in the air, flitting about, not grounded, it means to be anxious, it means to be in a constant state of anxiety. It's directly related to the anxiety around not having enough.

It's remarkable, if you think about it: we're among the wealthiest people in the history of the world, living in one of the wealthiest nations the world has ever known. And yet we are living in a culture driven by a sense of scarcity. It's everywhere, this "never enough" obsession: never good enough, perfect enough, thin enough, rich enough, powerful enough, successful enough, smart enough, certain enough, safe enough, extraordinary enough.[2] Scarcity. The word comes from the Old Norman French *scars*, meaning "restricted in quantity." "Scarcity thrives in a culture where everyone is hyperaware of *lack*. Everything from safety and love to money and resources feels restricted or lacking. We spend inordinate amounts of time calculating how much we have, want, and don't have, and how much everyone else has, needs, and wants."[3]

Brené Brown is a sociologist at the University of Texas. Her research is confirming what many theologians have said for years: it's very destructive living with a sense of scarcity, especially when it's not really true. In fact, her data shows that "worrying about scarcity is our culture's version of post-traumatic stress." The world has never been an easy place, but what Brown is finding in her analysis of our society, including numerous interviews with people, is that the "past decade has been traumatic for so many people that it's made changes in our culture. From 9/11, multiple wars, and the recession, to catastrophic natural disasters and the increase in random violence and school shootings, we've survived and are surviving events that have torn at our sense of safety with such force that we've experienced them as trauma even"—and this is significant!—even "if we weren't directly involved."[4]

As psychologists know, you can still be traumatized even if you're not directly impacted by a traumatic event. The sense of anxiety is also fueled by 24-hour news channels that are always giving us something more to worry about. And

---

[2] Brené Brown, *Daring Greatly: How the Courage to Be Vulnerable Transforms the Way We Live, Love, Parent, and Lead* (Gotham Books, 2012), 25.
[3] Brown, 26. Emphasis added.
[4] Brown, 27.

so the sense of anxiety and scarcity builds and builds and reaches a critical mass and people start to make decisions and make choices based on the perception of scarcity. People make choices and decisions from *within* their anxiety, caught up in worry. Anxiety drives our decisions, our reactions, our choices.

Stop striving for more. God knows what you need. Don't worry. Robert Frost (1874-1963) once said, "The reason why worry kills more people than work is because more people worry than work."

If you want to strive for something, if you want a job to do, if you want something to focus your anxiety on and allay your fears, then "strive for God's kingdom," Jesus says, "and these things"—meaning life, food, clothing, everything else—"will be given to you as well."

According to Jesus, the antidote to worry is the *kingdom*. The kingdom is the core message of Jesus' preaching. Now, it's natural to be anxious and to worry. But Jesus wants us to direct our attention away from what we think we don't have (scarcity) to what we already do have, which is God's kingdom that is and is still coming, and then he reminds us and calls us to rest and trust in God's providential care for *all* of creation, from the detestable ravens, to the lilies of the field, to every human being created in God's image. For we are, as the psalmist said, the apple of God's eye (Psalm 17:8). Jesus is drawing us out away from anxious obsessions toward God's faithfulness and invites us to act from within that sense of trust. *To be caught up in a constant state of anxiety and worry is lack of faith.* In other words, it's a sign that we're not fully resting in God's goodness. I don't think Jesus says this to judge us—nor do I say this in judgment—Jesus isn't trying to make our lives more difficult, but wants to show us a still more excellent way.

Seek God's kingdom. Strive after the kingdom. Try putting your energy and resources and time and even your anxieties into *kingdom work*. Where is the kingdom? Open your eyes! Consider! See, it's all around you! The kingdom is not "up there," "not in some heaven light-years away."[5] It's here. It's now. And it's coming; it's on the way. And what is kingdom work?

Works of mercy.
Works of peace.
Works of restorative justice.
Suffering for the things that really matter.
Works of reconciliation.
Works of redemption.

---

[5] From Marty Haugen's hymn "Gather Us In." *Sing the Faith* (Louisville: Geneva Press, 2003).

Works of radical, irrational generosity, of sharing—not grasping and grabbing, but giving joyfully because there's more than enough to go around.

Works of struggle and liberation on behalf of those who are poor, weak, and hungry, and naked, and alone, and scared, without voice, without power, without influence.

Works of wholeness and healing for all God's children (of all ages), children who don't know yet that they're worth more than the birds, who don't know yet they are beloved children of God.

Works of joy. Works of faith. Works of hope. Works of love.

This—and more—is what we're called to strive after. When we confess to one another or to the wider world that we are followers of Jesus Christ, we are saying that this is our work, too: at home, at work, at play, at church. This is our work. This is who we are. Can we accept this? Or is this all easier said than done?

Well, if we still have the need to worry over something, if we can't break the habit, then let the church worry over the things that matter, the kingdom and the coming of the kingdom. This, Jesus said, is the pearl of great price (Matthew 13:46). For where our treasure is, there will our hearts be also (Luke 12:34).

More Light, More Truth

John 16:12-15
Trinity Sunday

Sometimes our maps are wrong. Here's a story about such a map, the Martellus Map.

Henricus Martellus is the Latinized name of Heinrich Hammer. Hammer was a geographer and cartographer from Nuremberg, Germany, who lived and worked in Florence from 1480 to 1496. Between 1489 and 1491, he produced a map of the known world, an enormous map, measuring four feet by six feet, designed to hang on a wall. There's only one copy of it, which was discovered in 1960 and then donated to the Beinecke Rare Book and Manuscript Library at Yale University. It has a fascinating history. Portions of the map were borrowed from Ptolemy (90-168), the Greco-Egyptian polymath, who mapped the world around the year 150. Martellus' descriptions of Asia were informed by the writings of Marco Polo (1254-1324). Martellus also used a map produced in Lisbon, in 1485, by Bartolemeo Columbus (c. 1461-1515), Christopher's brother. In fact, Christopher Columbus used the Martellus map to persuade Ferdinand of Aragon (1462-1516) and Isabella of Castille (1451-1504) to support his desire to find a shorter and faster trade route to the East, in order to bypass the not always welcoming Ottoman Empire.

The big question, for both the Spanish monarchs and Columbus, was this: is it three thousand or ten thousand miles from Europe to Japan? Martellus based his drawings on Ptolemy's calculation of the size of the earth (the Greeks had already measured the circumference of the earth within about a few hundred miles), combined with knowledge gained from Marco Polo's travels through Asia. Martellus incorrectly placed Japan about one thousand miles off the coast of China—he assumed that there was nothing between Japan and the Iberian Peninsula except the Atlantic Ocean, thus he exaggerated the size of Asia to make up the difference. The map that Columbus used, the Martellus map, suggested that Japan was closer to Spain than it really was. And there was something else neither Columbus nor anyone else suspected—that an enormous land mass was there in between, the Americas, which some of us call home. When "Columbus sailed the ocean blue in 1492" and landed in the Bahamas he thought he was in Japan. It's remarkable, looking back, that the learned of that day could not imagine something other than what was expected.

Sometimes our maps are wrong. We create them with the best available knowledge, thinking we're being scientific, but there always seems to be a bias built in. We make assumptions about what is and is not true, about what can or cannot be true. Even GPS systems and our Smartphones are not always smart. Sometimes the maps are wrong. I read this week about a driver in Ontario who blindly followed her GPS system, through the fog, and drove straight into Lake Huron. The car sank and she swam to shore. Whether it's Martellus' map of the then known world or the maps of our personal lives, sometimes our maps are wrong—there's a lot that's unknown.

Yes, the map was wrong—as Columbus discovered—but that didn't prevent him (and others after him) from further exploration into the unknown. They used the map, but didn't trust it completely because they knew they were first *explorers* and *discovers* and only second mapmakers trying to map the unknown world. Maps were often drawn and then redrawn and then redrawn again after experience either confirmed or discounted what they suspected to be true. For example, there was a myth floating around in the sixteenth and seventeenth centuries that California was actually floating, that it was an island. In 1747 King Ferdinand VI (1713-1759) of Spain made a formal decree, "California [is] not an island," as it had been assumed (due to an error in previous maps). It's part of the mainland. Even up to the American Revolution this myth was out there in America and Europe.

In his book *Failure of Nerve*, Edwin Friedman (who was an expert on leadership and change dynamics in families, organizations, institutions, and religious communities) argues that Columbus' voyage was a hinge event, a turning point in the history of the world, for a variety of reasons. This discovery catapulted Europe out of a kind of cultural depression; it metabolized new energy and creativity. It transformed the world and what individuals considered possible. Friedman writes, "For a fundamental reorientation to occur, that human spirit of adventure which epitomizes serendipity and which enables new perceptions beyond the control of our thinking processes must happen first."[1]

The spirit of adventure is needed. It's easy to get stuck in faulty patterns of perception and behavior. We become gridlocked, when what we really need is to break free from the grid.

We Presbyterians love our order. We have our blessed *Book of Order* and an Order of Worship, and we love to quote the Apostle Paul, when he admonishes the Corinthians, "Let everything be done decently and in order" (1 Corinthians 14:40). Back in the 1980s, I once had a t-shirt made at the mall

---

[1] Edwin W. Friedman, *The Failure of Nerve: Leadership in the Age of the Quick Fix* (Seabury Books, 2007).

that read: *Presbyterians Do It Decently and in Order.* Looking back on that now, that was really odd! I was an odd teenager. I can only imagine what the guy at the mall was thinking. He had difficulty spelling the word *Presbyterian.*

Reflecting on our obsession for order today, I wonder if, perhaps, what we really need is more *disorder*, something to break us out of what confines the Church today. It's tough for me to admit this as one who is *very* Presbyterian. I don't really know what I'm suggesting or know what more disorder would look like, but I suspect it's true. Yes, of course, order is needed for the Spirit to move. The Spirit does move in and through order. But the Spirit also moves through disorder. Sometimes the Spirit even creates the disorder! She *intentionally* stirs things up—probably to show us that we're wrong and that we need to change!

Humility of knowledge. Maybe that's what we need today. Humility of knowledge. I'm always struck by the power of human arrogance, when we think we know more than we really do, and how this attitude hinders progress, and then gets us into a lot of trouble, and produces a lot of pain and suffering. The word *humility* literally means, from the Latin *humus*, "of the earth." Humility means being "of the earth," in other words, being grounded, real, honest, truthful. Humility of knowledge means being real, honest about what we know and don't know. Humility of knowledge checks hubris, it keeps us humble, but it also reminds us that there's more to learn and discover in the world.

This is certainly true for science. Jeff Bolognese, a member of Catonsville Presbyterian Church, shared with me recently, when we were touring NASA Goddard, that most scientists are actually very humble in acknowledging what they don't know, and they are often blown away by new discoveries about the universe, which then pushes them to want to discover even more. Consider how our views of the universe have changed because of the Hubble telescope.

What is true of science is also true of theology, which was one time known as the Queen of the Sciences. Humility of knowledge is especially needed among Christians today, needed within the Church. Yes, we need to confess our faith, know what we believe and why. But we also need to confess our doubt and honor our doubt as an expression of our faith, as odd as that might sound. We also need to be humble enough to acknowledge how much we don't know about God, about Christ, about the Holy Spirit, about what it means to really be a disciple of Jesus Christ. Each and every one of us needs to acknowledge that there's still so much to learn! This might freak out our Fundamentalist friends, but it's true. There's more than one interpretation of a biblical text. Scholars are always learning more about the meaning of an obscure Hebrew or Greek word, uncovering more about the composition of ancient texts, making new archeological discoveries that alter how we read and hear a text.

There's so much to learn! We need a spirit of adventure and discovery within the Church today, a bold spirit that will allow us to set sail from the old world into a new world of faithfulness; we need the courage to venture from the known out into the unknown.

The novelist Joseph Conrad (1857-1924) tells us that as boy he loved to look at maps. "I would look for hours at South America, or Africa, or Australia, and lose myself in all the glories of exploration. At that time there were many blank spaces on the earth, and when I saw one that looked particularly inviting on a map (but they all look like that) I would put my finger on it and say, When I grow up I will go there." Two decades later, in 1890, Conrad wrote *Heart of Darkness* and exposed the violence and brutal suffering in the Belgian Congo.

Walt Whitman (1818-1892) captured this spirit of adventure in *Leaves of Grass*, using the experience of traveling at sea as a metaphor for life:

> O we can wait no longer,
> We too take ship O soul,
> Joyous we too launch out on trackless seas,
> Fearless for unknown shores on waves of ecstasy to sail,
> Amid the wafting winds, (thou pressing me to thee, I thee to me, O soul,)
> Caroling free, singing our song of God,
> Chanting our chant of pleasant exploration.
> ...
> Away O soul! hoist instantly the anchor!
> Cut the hawsers—haul out—shake out every sail!
> ...
> Sail forth—steer for the deep waters only!
> Reckless O soul, exploring, I with thee, and thou with me,
> For we are bound where mariner has not yet dared to go,
> And we will risk the ship, ourselves and all.[2]

What would that spirit of adventure mean for the Church today, for *this* church, for our individual lives? Before the pilgrims left for Plymouth, in 1620, the Rev. John Robinson (1576-1625), known as the "pastor of the pilgrims," offered a Farewell Speech in Delfshaven. He said, famously, "I am verily persuaded the Lord hath more truth and light to break forth from his

---

[2] Walt Whitman, from "Passage to India," *Leaves of Grass* (1900).

holy Word." This is an extremely significant affirmation, if you think about it. These pilgrims or religious separatists, these Calvinist Christians, our theological forbears, are about to leave the safety of home to venture to an unknown place, a dangerous place, crossing an ocean, all because their theological convictions were calling them to go *forward*. It wasn't a backward spirit driving them, but a forward movement. Robinson also said in the speech that we must not look back toward the reformers, to Luther and Calvin, but to discover things they couldn't see.[3] Significantly, as good Reformed Christians, people who are reformed and always being reformed, by the Word and the Spirit, they trust, they know that there's still so much to learn and discover and explore in the life of faith.

God's Word is dynamic. It's not static. To cite the tagline for the United Church of Christ, "God is still speaking." (I wish we Presbyterians had a similar tagline!) If God is still speaking then we need to listen, which also requires humility because we can't expect to know what God will say before God speaks. We need to be quiet long enough to listen and not assume what will be said. Listening requires courage, courage to acknowledge what is heard and then, guided by the Spirit, courage to set sail, to step out, to lean in, to act, to move.

Yes, all of this is anxiety producing. All of this is scary. Of course it is! Who said the life of faith is about being safe? Jesus never said, "Follow me and I will make you safe." We're not called to play it safe. Safety has little or nothing to do with it.

The Word, God's creative Word speaking *through* the pages of scripture, still has so much to teach us! We don't have it all figured out. Biblical scholars are always being humbled by what they don't know. For example, the 1946 discovery of the Dead Sea Scrolls in Qumran, which date from Jesus' lifetime, along with the 1945 discovery of the Gospel of Thomas, in the Egyptian desert, a text that might predate the Gospel of Mark, have and are changing what we know.

There's always more to explore, more to discover, more to fathom and understand. Didn't Jesus say that when the "Spirit of truth comes; he will guide [us] into all the truth" (John 16:12)? The Holy Spirit still has much to teach us. I find it striking that the disciples didn't learn everything they needed for being disciples when Jesus was with them. It wasn't as if they had three years of seminary with Jesus, and then he sent them off to change the world.

---

[3] John Robinson's Farewell Speech, 1620, "The Lutherans cannot be drawn to go beyond what Luther saw. Whatever part of His will our God has revealed to Calvin, they (Lutherans) will rather die than embrace it; and the Calvinists, you see, stick fast where they were left by that great man of God, who yet saw not all things. This is a misery much to be lamented."

There was still more to learn after his departure. Perhaps they weren't wise enough or strong enough or humble enough to learn those things during Jesus' life, to enter into "all the truth" at that time. Perhaps their hearts weren't deep enough or open enough to fully fathom the truth of God's love and grace.

The same is certainly true of us today. The Spirit is still the guide and the teacher and the source of truth, who reveals and discloses to us things beyond our imagining, things beyond our seeing (1 Corinthians 2:6-10), beyond reason, things beyond the limited confines of what we know, whose wisdom leads us forward. We have yet to figure out what it means to really follow Christ, to bear the name *Christian*. We have yet to fully fathom the heights and the depths of God's grace and what is being asked of us with our lives. Our hearts need to be as deep and wide as the oceans of God's love. We have yet to discover what it means when we pray "Thy kingdom come, thy will be done, on earth as it is in heaven"—we certainly haven't arrived at that new world, that kingdom world. But that's where the Spirit wants to take us, is taking us, will take us, is willing to guide us every step along the way, even if we don't have a map, even if our maps are wrong. Trust the Spirit.

George Macleod (1895-1991) of the Iona Community said, "Christians are explorers, not mapmakers." We're *explorers*. We're called to explore and then revise the maps of God's grace and justice and love, so that others coming after us will find a way, so that they may then go beyond us—because there's still so much to discover!

Dreaming the Dream Forward

John 2:1-11

Well, that was quite a wedding, wasn't it? Don't you wish you were on that guest list? Wouldn't you have loved to be on the guest list? It was quite the party. Everyone was there. The disciples were there and Jesus and his mother, who bossed Jesus about. And lots of wine was consumed, so much they ran out of it, no doubt embarrassing the host. That's probably why Mary told Jesus, the ever-responsible one, to do something about it.

Having wine at a wedding was a sign of generosity and hospitality. Wine didn't flow freely in Jesus' time. It was a cash crop, like olive oil. The poor drank little wine. They drank water with their daily diet of cheese and bread and olive oil. Weddings were different. The couple's family had to save for a long time in order to have wine at a wedding reception. Family and friends passed harsh judgments on those who couldn't throw a wedding in style.[1] The wine was supposed to flow freely. So there's shame here in Cana. The family couldn't afford enough wine for their guests. Mary tells Jesus to do something about it, and then she says to the servants, "Do whatever he tells you."

Jesus orders the servants to take the large, stone water jars used for purification, six of them, obviously empty, and fill them with water. They did as they were told, drew some out, and gave it to the wine steward who, unaware of the miracle, was impressed by the quality of the new wine. The steward says to the groom, "Everyone serves the good wine first, and then the inferior wine after the guests have become drunk. But you have kept the good wine until now" (John 2:10)." It's a sign, John tells us, Jesus' first sign.

Ah, but what does it signify? That's the question. This "miracle" story is highly symbolic. When we read John's gospel we need to remember that there are always two narratives, two levels of meaning, two stories going on at the same time. There's what's happening on the surface of things and then there's the deeper, more significant symbolic meaning. This is "just" a wedding that runs out of wine. I'm sure that happened all the time. It's an ordinary domestic scene. And, yet, this miracle actually symbolizes something else for those with eyes to see. This text, like most of John's gospel, is swimming in symbolism. A surface reading of the story misses the point—which I'll get to shortly.

---

[1] Gerard Sloyan, *John* (Atlanta: John Knox Press, 1988), 36.

First, I'm struck by the way today's gospel lectionary beautifully complements the Martin Luther King, Jr. holiday this weekend. It might seem like a stretch to suggest that Jesus' miracle at Cana has anything to do with King's life and witness and struggle. But there's a connection. The text has something to say to the Church as we continue to dream the dream.

We know his famous "I Have a Dream" speech given on the steps of the Lincoln Memorial at the March on Washington for Jobs and Freedom on August 28, 1963. We've seen photos of that event. Seen the film footage. Perhaps you were there. Whenever I visit the Lincoln Memorial (my favorite monument in DC), I'm always struck by the juxtaposition of the massive statute of Lincoln, with the Gettysburg Address carved into the wall to Lincoln's right and the Second Inaugural Address to his left, one of the most theologically profound addresses ever given by a president. Whenever I'm there, I look for the stone marker at the top of the steps that indicates the exact spot Dr. King offered his speech, with Lincoln looking over his shoulder. "I have a dream," he said, "that one day this nation will rise up and live out the true meaning of its creed: 'We hold these truths to be self-evident, that all men are created equal.'"[2] One day.

Two days after the speech, the COINTELPRO, a covert program of the FBI, which at times acted beyond the law, said, "In the light of King's powerful demagogic speech yesterday he stands head and shoulders above all other Negro leaders put together when it comes to influencing great masses of Negroes. We must mark him now, if we have not done so before, as the most dangerous Negro of the future in this Nation from the standpoint of communism, the Negro and national security."[3]

There was much suffering and pain and death in the years following that speech. And, thank God, we have come far, very far, since the days of segregation and Jim Crow. It was said with the election of Barack Obama as president that we entered into a post-racial America. I didn't believe that in 2008, and I certainly don't believe that now.

It's all too painfully obvious to us, especially in light of recent events in Ferguson, New York, Charleston, Chicago, and right here in Baltimore this year, that for many African-Americans, that dream is still "a dream deferred," to quote the poet Langston Hughes (1902-1967). King's "I Have a Dream"

---

[2] Full text of his speech may be found here: https://www.archives.gov/press/exhibits/dream-speech.pdf.
[3] Memo hosted by American Radio Works (American Public Media), "The FBI's War on King."

speech was actually connected to a poem by Hughes, written in 1951, called "Harlem." It goes like this:

> What happens to a dream deferred?
> Does it dry up/ like a raisin in the sun?
> Or fester like a sore—And then run?
> Does it stink like rotten meat?
> Or crust and sugar over—like a syrupy sweet?
> Maybe it just sags
> like a heavy load.
> Or does it explode?[4]

It's a good question.

Maybe there's a problem with the dream itself? Some might say, "Well, what King offered was only a dream," meaning it was a "fantasy," it wasn't realistic. "It raised expectations that can't be fully realized in American society. It's nice to be optimistic, imagine a future, but don't get carried away." Some contemporary authors, such as Ta-Nehisi Coates, who grew up in West Baltimore, seems to suggest in his recent bestselling *Between the World and Me*, a series of letters to his son, that King's dream, rooted in the Judaic-Christian vision of justice and redemption, along with the American dream, are both illusions, at least for African-Americans. Struggle, he says. Stop dreaming.[5]

Unfortunately, people don't put a lot of stock in their dreams, in the power of dreams to transform us and change us. Some, such as Sigmund Freud (1856-1939), think our dream life is a big trash compactor that processes all the stuff from our waking life. Others, such as Carl Jung, believed that dreams are given by the psyche, maybe even by God, to compensate for the extremes of our waking life, to offer balance. Dreams can also have a prospective dimension to them; their message originates from some deep place, often with a greater wisdom and generosity than our skittish, frightful egos. These dreams call for action, for change. They move us forward; they lead us toward transformation and wholeness. Jung also believed that profound dreams, "big dreams," can be lived and relived in order to fathom their meaning and depth.[6] Dreams can be a kind of North Star that lead us in the way we should go. From this perspective, we need to dream the dream forward, or, better, live the dream forward. I'm firmly in Jung's camp here.

---

[4] Langston Hughes, "Harlem," *Selected Poems of Langston Hughes* (Random House, 1990).
[5] Ta-Nehesi Coates, *Between the World and* Me (New York: Spiegel & Grau, 2015).
[6] See C. G. Jung, "General Aspects of Dream Psychology," *The Structure and Dynamics of the Psyche, The Collected Works of C. G. Jung*, Vol. 8 (Princeton: Princeton University Press, 1981).

King's dream, his vision still needs to be lived forward. We've made great strides. But as they sing at the end of the musical *Hairspray*, "I know we've come so far, but [baby, baby] we've got so far to go."[7] There's still so much work that needs to be done.

Throughout King's ministry the dream was expressed in his vision of the Beloved Community. King said, "Our goal is to create a beloved community and this will require a qualitative change in our souls as well as a quantitative change in our lives."[8] His words resound with the gospel; they echo Jesus' teaching on the Kingdom of God (or Kin-dom or Realm, even Empire of God). The beloved community is the dream—a dream that shapes our waking life. And if we're going to enter into that community, if we are going to live from the dream, if we're really going to get there and are serious about wanting to get there, it will only come through *change*: qualitative change in our individual souls, in our hearts, change in the nature of our thoughts and feelings and quantitative change in our lives, in our actions, collective action strong enough that moves us off from dead center or the way things are. The *status quo* is often *status woe*, especially for those without power or privilege.

Why is it so difficult for us, both as a Church and as a nation, to talk honestly and openly about racism? We all struggle with this, whether we're black or white or neither. Whether it's the sin of racism in our past or the consequences of the unconfessed sin of racism that plagues our present, we need to be honest about it. Racism is sin, and every institution—church, nation, corporation, family—that benefits from being racist or helps to support racism is in sin, is caught in sin, is a partner in crime against the human spirit. It's why Jim Wallis, of the evangelical-social justice Sojourners community, calls racism America's "original sin."[9] Philosopher Eddie Glaude, Jr., who teaches at Princeton University just released a book this week with the title *Democracy in Black: How Race Still Enslaves the American Soul*.

Until we confess the sin of racism, both as a people and as individuals, and acknowledge our own complicity in it—no matter how difficult and painful it is to do so—and then repent, which means changing our hearts and our minds and actions, both individually and collectively, nothing will change. Christians have to act. Christians have to call out other Christians when they're being racist. Christians need to confess their complicity in the sin of slavery.

---

[7] *Hairspray*, music by Marc Shaiman and lyrics by Scott Wittman, 2002.
[8] Martin Luther King, Jr., *Nonviolence: The Only Road to Freedom*, May 4, 1966).
[9] Jim Wallis, *America's Original Sin: Racism, White Privilege, and the Bridge to a New America* (Brazos, 2016).

Christian culture isn't innocent. We helped to cause the mess we're in. The first slave ship to arrive on these shores in 1564, a British vessel, was named "The Goodship Jesus."[10] Ta-Nehisi writes to his son, "You cannot forget how much they took from us and how they transfigured our very bodies into sugar, tobacco, cotton, and gold."[11] History is never destiny, though. The Church must be able to embody the change and transformation that it teaches. If the Church, of all places, can't be a model for reconciliation, if we can't change ourselves and bring about the change, then what are we here for?

Why is it so difficult? I was recently reminded of W. H. Auden's (1907-1973) searing words:

> We would rather be ruined than changed
> We would rather die in our dread
> Than climb the cross of the moment
> And let our illusions die.[12]

We can't do this ourselves. That's why the water is changed into wine. There is no way for the followers of Jesus to follow him and claim his name without change. Sure, the wedding guests needed wine. So Jesus made wine. But there's another level of meaning in this story that says something about what matters most to Jesus and those who love him. To trust in him means that we will undergo change and experience change until we die. And we need to change. We need to be transformed. The entire Christian life is all about ongoing change and reform. Those six stone jars were originally made only to hold water, water for purification. They must now be put to a different use. "The water of one era must be replaced by the wine of another."[13]

Wine, itself, in this story is symbolic of the New Age, it's the New Way that Jesus offers the world. It's a sign of the Messianic Age. In the book of First Enoch, written before Jesus' time, we're told "in those days," the Messianic Age, the vines will produce wine in plenitude. Philo the Jew (25 BC-50 AD) of Alexandria, a contemporary of Jesus, spoke of God's presence in the world in terms of rich, red wine. Curiously, this comes from Philo's treatise called *On Dreams*. Jesus provides wine, loads of wine, about 180 gallons of the finest wine! This revealed his glory "and his disciples believed in him" (John 2:11).

If Jesus can do that to water, just imagine what he is doing and wants to do with us and for us—we who are mostly water. *We* need to be made into new

---

[10] Coates, 71.
[11] Cited in Howard Thurman, *Jesus and the Disinherited* (Boston: Beacon Press, 1976), 14.
[12] W. H. Auden, "Age of Anxiety" (1948).
[13] Sloyan, 39.

wine ourselves: something needs to occur within us. *We* are supposed to embody God's New Order, God's New Age, God's Kingdom.

Dr. King's dream wasn't King's dream. It was and is *God's* dream and we need to allow God's dream to dream *through* us, to dream us forward, allow God's dream to shape us and to change us—into new wine.

Always Reforming

2 Corinthians 5:16-6:10
Reformation Sunday

Sola scriptura. Sola gratia. Sola fide. Solus Christus. Soli Deo gloria. These are the Five Solae, five Latin phrases that together sum up the core theological vision of the Protestant Reformation. *Scripture alone. Grace alone. Faith alone. Christ alone. Glory to God alone.* The pillars of the Reformation. They represent the broad theological tenets that emerged throughout the Church's Reformation in the early sixteenth century. Each one is a counter claim, that is, a rejection of prevailing theological views of the Roman Catholic Church at the time. Scripture alone has authority, not tradition. Grace, faith, alone, not works righteousness. Christ, not the Pope. God's glory, not the glory of the Church or the glory of humanity. These were the beliefs that rocked and then split the Church in the early 1500s, unleashing a movement of reform that the Church had never witnessed before or since.

Today, as Presbyterians, as a people reformed, we are heirs of this movement. On the 31st of October 1517, in Wittenberg, Germany, when Martin Luther (1483-1536) posted ninety-five reasons why the Church should not be involved in the sale of indulgences, he never dreamed we would be remembering him these many years later. Indulgences were basically certificates one could buy to release a loved one from the confines of purgatory. One of the indulgence sellers, Johann Tetzel (1465-1519) even came up with a little jingle: "When the coin in the copper rings, the soul from purgatory springs." The proceeds were used to build St. Peter's Basilica in Rome. When Luther protested the sale of indulgences, he didn't anticipate centuries later we would be honoring his act of conscience.

On Reformation Sunday, the Sunday closest to the 31st of October, Protestants around the world celebrate and remember the reformers: Luther in Germany, Jean Cauvin (1509-1564) in Geneva, Ülrich Zwingli (1484-1531) and Heinrich Bullinger (1504-1574) in Zurich, John Knox (c. 1514-1572) in St. Andrews and Edinburgh, Scotland. We remember their passion, their commitment, their courage, their love for the gospel and need to reform the church.

If I could give you a walking tour of St. Andrews, I would take you to two places in particular. I would show you to the ruin of the bishop's castle and invite you to look down at the pavement and see two letters: GW. And then I would take you to St. Salvator's, the University Chapel. In the cobbles outside the chapel are two letters: PH. These are the initials of two men, George Wishart (1513-1546) and Patrick Hamilton (1504-1528), who were burned at the stake for their reforming ideas.

One of my favorite places in St. Andrews is the hill situated along the North Sea where the Martyrs Monument stands. Inscribed on it are the names of the reformers who died for their faith in St. Andrews. Whenever I'm back there I always make a point of going to the monument. I find a bench and reflect on their witness. I think of their courage, their dedication to the gospel of Jesus Christ, what they experienced, their commitment to these beliefs—*sola scriptura, sola gatia, sola fide, solus Christos, soli Deo gloria*—and I ask, could I, would I do the same? Would you? Could you?

In 2017 we will mark the 500th anniversary of the Reformation. Almost five hundred years on, the spirit of reform is still alive, particularly in China and many nations in Africa. But to be honest, in the West it's losing steam. I've been to Geneva, the city of Calvin, twice. The Protestant ethos is there in the people and the architecture, but the churches are empty, as is true for most places in Europe. Iain Torrance, who preached in this pulpit several years ago, former president of Princeton Seminary, former moderator of the Church of Scotland, and now professor at New College, Edinburgh, said several years ago that Reformed Christianity (the heirs of Calvin) has lost its way. We have lost our vision.

For several years now, I've felt that something is seriously wrong with the Reformed tradition. It's been difficult to put a finger on it. It's more a sense, an intuition that something is missing. Personally, to be completely honest, I've come to feel that Christianity is in trouble. Yes, there are healthy and vibrant churches. I give thanks to God for churches such as this one, and many others like it, churches that are vital, engaged, and alive. I don't want to be pessimistic or negative, but you need to know that what we have here at CPC isn't the norm. So many churches are struggling to survive, many are plagued by conflict (just ask a presbytery executive or a Committee on Ministry chairperson), many have lost their focus, burnout rates among pastors are very high, and seminaries are struggling as enrollment continues to decline.

Several years ago, Dorothy Boulton (our associate pastor at the Catonsville Church) returned from a visit to London. She spent a day visiting Oxford and showed me a photo of a sign situated at the entrance to the chapel of Christ Church College. It reads: "What is the church?" The sign provides a description of Christian worship and beliefs. Now, think about this for a minute. You don't have to explain what a church *is* if people already know. And you don't have to explain what goes on *in* church if people are actually going to church, if they're part of a church. The sign is itself a symbol, a symbol that points to the deeper, pervasive reality that the Church is becoming (has already become?) a relic from another time.

I'm not trying to be negative or pessimistic. Believe me. What the Church needs, however, is a healthy dose of realism. So what do we do? We can celebrate our past, I guess. We can commemorate the Reformation, reaffirm our beliefs—teach our children well—remember what makes us Protestants.

There was a time when I thought knowing what we believe and why was enough. There was a time when I thought getting the ideas right, getting the theology right was the cure for what ails the Church. After twenty-five years of ministry, I'm not so sure. Don't get me wrong: ideas matter, theology matters. As we know, there's a lot of loopy theology out there in the Church these days.

What I've come to know is this: *Tending belief is high maintenance.* Beliefs require verification, right? And then proof, right? And argument. And then they require protection, right? We have to defend them. *Welcome to the belligerent world of beliefs!* What I've found in the belligerent world of beliefs is that often the beliefs we fight about have very little to do with the reality of God. Instead, we're often dealing with embattled egos, beliefs as extensions of *frightened* egos, beliefs used as weapons by frightened egos against people who appear threatening. *All of this has absolutely nothing to do with the gospel of Jesus Christ.*

The world has grown tired of beliefs. The world knows the costly price of dogmatic assertions and fundamentalisms of every kind. And the world has lost faith, is quickly losing faith in what the Church believes because the Church has failed to truly embody it—incarnate it, enflesh it—in its practice.

I, too, have grown tired, very tired of beliefs. Sounds odd coming from a preacher, right? That's how I feel.

The first Jesus followers did not have a belief system. Jesus called people to follow him, which meant more than believing in him, more than simply confessing certain theological ideas *about* him, and certainly more than an anemic ethical do-goodism (which often passes as "Christian" these days). The first followers of Christ had an experience of the holy, an encounter with the divine; they participated in the power and grace and intensity of God's Spirit unleashed upon the world in a new way, *gospel-ing* creation in the flesh, in a person, in Jesus Christ, who calls humanity to embark, like him, on a heroic journey of divine dimensions and cosmic proportions! That was the Apostle Paul's experience too. *Whatever Paul came to believe* about *Christ was first experienced* in *and* with *and* through *Christ and what he continued to experience through the Spirit.*

These are the rich, theological claims we find in 2 Corinthians. This is Paul at his finest, with soaring rhetoric and sublime theology. "So, if anyone is in Christ, there is a new creation; everything old has passed away; see, everything has become new! All this is from God, who reconciled us to himself through Christ and has given us the ministry of reconciliation; that is, in Christ, God was reconciling the world to himself, not counting their trespasses against them, and entrusting the message of reconciliation to us" (2 Cor. 5:17-19).

Let's go deeper into this text. We can dissect this text, isolate its theological claims, all the *beliefs* of the church: new creation, reconciliation, ministry. We can go deeper and say something about God's relationship with Christ, Christ's relationship with God, something about the doctrine of atonement, how God dealt with sin. Implied here, too, is Paul's understanding of the cross, salvation, and resurrection. All of this (and more!) is going on in 2 Corinthians 5:16-21. We can "mine" these verses for their theological claims, come up with a list of what one might believe about the faith. To approach the text only this way misses the point. It misses what's *behind* these theological claims. Go deeper still to what's behind the text, which is Paul's own life-experience, what he came to know through his own encounter with the Risen Christ. And this encounter didn't happen once but again and again throughout his life.

Hear again verse 21, "For our sake he made him to be sin who knew no sin, so that in him we might become the righteousness of God." Did you hear that? "...that *in him* we might become the righteousness of God." And now listen again to 6:1, "As we work together with him, we urge you also not to accept the grace of God in vain." Did you hear that? "...As we work together *with him*, we urge you ... not to accept the grace of God in vain."

And then Paul continues to talk about the nature of his ministry, a life that flows from an experience of God's grace, not from trust in ideas or beliefs. His wasn't a ministry of defending ideas or beliefs, but one urged on by the love of Christ. It's a life, a ministry that, right now, *participates* in the presence of the Risen Christ, who enabled Paul to undergo "great endurance, in afflictions, hardships, calamities, beatings, imprisonments, riots, labors, sleepless nights, hunger: by purity, knowledge, patience, kindness, holiness of spirit, genuine love, truthful speech, and the power of God" (2 Cor. 6:4-7). And I should note that "knowledge" here is not "theoretical understanding of theological propositions" but a deep, personal awareness of what Paul is being called to do.¹

The Reformed tradition has never been comfortable with personal experience. We prefer our rational, theological systems; we prefer to think our way to faith. We are a people of creeds and confessions. Don't get me wrong: there's a place for all of these. *But if beliefs hinder us from actually experiencing the grace that we, as Protestants, say actually saves, then something is missing. Something is terribly, seriously wrong.* Even Calvin, known for his methodical, systematic thinking, developed as his personal symbol the image of an upturned hand, an open palm holding a heart with a flame above it: a heart set on fire offered up to God, "Promptly and Sincerely."² Even Calvin, Mr. Cerebral Theologian that he was, knew that unless the gospel is inwardly digested, made real in hearts, as well as minds, the gospel remains at a distance from us, far away.

The gospel needs to penetrate the psyche, become part of who we are, shape how we see the world; it needs to be embodied in our lives. Without this our theological beliefs are just crafty cerebrations that do little to transform lives. And if our lives aren't transformed, if we ourselves aren't reforming and always being reformed by the Spirit of God, then how on earth can we be expected to help reform the world?

That's why these days I'm reading less theology and more psychology, specifically the work of the Swiss psychiatrist Carl G. Jung. (I'm slowly starting to write a book on Jung and Christian experience.) However, this isn't an academic exercise for me. I believe that Jung has a lot to offer the contemporary Church; he has a lot to say about how we view Christian experience.

Jung was truly one of the seminal geniuses of the twentieth century. One reason he's so relevant to us is because he himself was a child of the manse. His father was a Reformed pastor. Carl came from a long line of Reformed pastors and professors. He learned the catechism from his father; he read widely from his father's library, he was confirmed in the church. But when he first partook of Communion as an adolescent, he said it was a lifeless experience, both for him and seemingly everyone else sitting around him. Jung knew that his father was depressed, and he lost the zeal of his faith. His father knew the creeds, knew the beliefs of the church, regurgitated them in sermons week after week, but they didn't touch the depths of his soul. Carl,

---

[1] Ernest Best, *Second Corinthians-Interpretation: A Bible Commentary for Teaching and Preaching* (Louisville: John Knox Press, 1987), 61.
[2] Calvin's personal motto: "I offer my heart to thee O Lord, promptly and sincerely." (*Cor Meum Tibi Offero Domine Prompte Et Sincere*).

himself, had profound religious experiences as a child. He always had a fire in his belly for the divine. Jung eventually collaborated with Sigmund Freud (1856-1939) in the emerging field of psychoanalysis, but in the end it was the question of religion, the experience of the holy, the numinous, that led to their painful break. Freud wanted nothing to do with religion (he saw it as a source of neurosis); for Jung, the psyche was and is essentially religious.[3]

The last thirty years of Jung's life were spent exploring the psychological aspects of Christianity. He was very critical of theologians. Jung knew then, in the 1930s, that the church was in trouble; he knew that Christianity was in trouble. So he approached Christianity as if it were a patient in need of therapy.[4] He wanted to help heal the church, heal Christianity. Why? Because he saw it as the best hope for humanity. And he wanted to help heal the Protestant soul, which he knew was sick, especially in Europe after the Second World War. The Protestant soul is still in need of deep healing.

In a famous interview with the BBC in 1959, Jung was asked, "Dr. Jung, do you believe in God." After pausing for a moment, he said, "I don't believe. I know."[5] *I know*—knowledge rooted in experience. Jung said, "The Churches stand for traditional and collective convictions which in the case of many of its adherents are no longer based on their own inner experience but on *unreflecting belief*, which is notoriously apt to disappear as soon as one begins thinking about it."[6] This is why Jung said that "Christian civilization has proved hollow to a terrifying degree: it is all veneer, but the inner man has remained untouched and therefore unchanged. His soul is out of key with his external beliefs; ...."[7]

The strongest indictment of Christianity was the fact that so-called "Christian" Europe tore itself apart, and the world with it, in not one but two cataclysmic world wars. "Christian education," Jung said, "has done all that is humanly possible, but it has not been enough. Too few people have

---

[3] See Carl G. Jung, *Memories, Dreams, Reflections*, Aniela Jaffé, editor (New York: Vintage Books, 2011).
[4] See Murray Stein, *Jung's Treatment of Christianity: The Psychotherapy of a Religious Tradition* (Chiron Publications, 1986).
[5] The 1959 BBC interview on "Face to Face," may be viewed here: https://www.youtube.com/watch?v=eTBs-2cloEI.
[6] C. G. Jung, "The Undiscovered Self (Present and Future)," *The Collected Works of C. G. Jung*, Vol. 10, (Princeton: Princeton University Press, 1978), §521.
[7] C. G. Jung, "Introduction to the Religious and Psychological Problems of Alchemy," *Psychology and Alchemy*, The Collected Works of C. G. Jung, Vol. 12 (Princeton: Princeton University Press, 1977), §12.

experienced the divine image as the innermost possession of their own souls. Christ only meets them from without, never from within the soul."[8]

Jung insisted, "The advocates of Christianity squander their energies in the mere preservation of what had come down to them, with no thought of building on their house and making it roomier."[9] I think Jung is right.

The Church of Jesus Christ is not a museum. We're not a historical preservation society. We're called to reform—to be reformed by the Spirit who is calling us to a new day. We need to become roomier, building new homes in which the human spirit can thrive. We're not called to preserve the past or live in the past. Christ is alive. Christ is at work within us, now.

It's in the soul, in the heart, in the core of our being where the reformation of God's love and grace must be experienced in radically new ways, in order for it to be seen in the world, in order for the world to be reformed all for the glory of God. "In Christ there is a new creation: everything old has passed away; see, everything has become new!" Reformed and always being reformed. When we experience the ongoing reforming power of God's grace—not just believe in it, but know it, feel it, experience it—then the Church will really have something profound and meaningful and relevant to offer the world again.

May it be so. *Amen.*

---

[8] C. G. Jung, *CW* 12, §12.
[9] C. G. Jung, *Aion: Researches into the Phenomenology of the Self, The Collected Works of C. G. Jung*, Vol. 9, ii, (Princeton: Princeton University Press, 1979), §170.

The Reconciliation of All Things

Colossians 1:11-20
Reign of Christ Sunday

On Friday, this nation remembered that tragic day in 1963 when President John F. Kennedy (1917-1963) was fatally shot in Dallas, bringing an end to Camelot. Fifty years. In the grand scheme of things, not very long ago. And yet, in many ways it was another age, another time, another world. This past week the press took us back to remember that fateful day and invited us to imagine how the world could have been different if November 22 was just another ordinary day in 1963. However, the press overlooked (for the most part) two other major figures who died that same day. One was the humanist, pacifist Aldous Huxley (1894-1963), a leading intellectual of his day and author of the *Brave New World*, a novel written in 1931 that envisioned the world in the year 2540. *Brave New World* was ranked among the top 100 novels of the twentieth century. Through an imaginary rendering of what the future will be, Huxley critiqued issues that faced Europe and the United States in 1930s, between the wars.

The other notable figure who died fifty years ago on November 22 was Clive Staples Lewis—C.S. Lewis (1898-1963), the Oxford don, scholar, medievalist, author of children's books such as *The Chronicles of Narnia*, and many volumes of Christian apologetics, with well-known titles, such as *The Screwtape Letters*, *God in the Dock*, and perhaps his most famous theological work, *Mere Christianity*. In his memoir *Surprised by Joy: The Shape of My Early Life*, Lewis told the story of his conversion from atheism to theism to his eventual trust and faith in Christ, calling himself "the most reluctant convert in all of England."

On Friday evening downtown at the meeting of the American Academy of Religion there was a celebration of Lewis's work and influence, led by N. T. Wright, the former bishop of Durham, now professor at the University of St. Andrews. Wright has been described as a kind of "Lewis" for our day, writing about Christianity to a broad audience. Wright is also one of the leading Pauline scholars in the world. He just published what will surely be a landmark book on the letters of Paul, a work—at more than 1700 pages—that will shape biblical scholarship for the next fifty years.[1]

---

1 On Tuesday, November 26, 2013, I attended a fascinating session at the American Academy of Religion, meeting in Baltimore, "Reflections on the Fiftieth Anniversary of the Death of C.S. Lewis," presided by my friend Robert MacSwain. Four papers were given by leading

More people are reading C.S. Lewis today than ever before. Children of all faiths (and none) are still hearing about the adventures of Peter, Susan, Edmund, and Lucy venturing through the magical wardrobe into the land Narnia, the world of the White Witch, and the powerful, never safe but always good Aslan, a character who symbolizes Christ.

What an imagination Lewis had. Lewis is a wonderful example of how imagination, particularly a Christian, that is, *baptized* imagination, images the world, figures and transfigured the world, envisions the world. He created a marvelous world for his characters, for us really, and in doing so allowed us to reimagine our world, to envision what is possible. By offering an alternative world, he transfigured the way we see the world and our lives within it. It's all the more remarkable, really, given that one time in a conversation about faith with J.R.R. Tolkien (1892-1973), over a pint of ale at the Eagle and Child pub in Oxford, Tolkien became increasingly frustrated with Lewis—who was still a non-believer at this point whereas Tolkien was a devout Roman Catholic—and said, "Your inability to understand stems from a failure of imagination on your part!" Can you imagine telling C.S. Lewis that he suffers from a failure of imagination?

My mentor at Princeton Seminary, James Loder (1931-2001)—who was also a huge C.S. Lewis fan and who sketched images of Aslan for his children—suggested that we need to make a distinction between the *imaginary* and the *imaginative*. Something that is imaginary takes you out of the world, out of reality; it's a flight of fancy, often escapist. An imaginative act, on the other hand, is an entirely different faculty. It was the Danish philosopher Søren Kierkegaard (1813-1855) who understood imagination as the capacity *instar omnium*, meaning equivalent to all in importance. As a faculty of the self, imagination has the capacity to create, order, and reorder the world. The imaginative act, thought, or word has the power to put you more deeply *into* the world, *into* a world transfigured, *into* the real.[2]

What does all of this have to do with Colossians 1 or with the Reign of Christ Sunday? A lot. Today is the last Sunday of the liturgical year, the way the Church orders its Sundays and patterns its worship upon Jesus' life, death, resurrection, and ascension. Next week is Advent, and we begin the annual cycle afresh. Next week we begin to wait. This week we lift up a different,

---

theologians and philosophers assessing Lewis's writings and his relevancy today. See also Robert MacSwain and Michael Ward, eds., *The Cambridge Companion to C.S. Lewis* (Cambridge: Cambridge University Press, 2010). See N. T. Wright, *Paul and the Faithfulness of God* (Minneapolis: Fortress Press, 2013).
[2] James E. Loder, *The Transforming Moment* (Colorado Springs: Helmers & Howard, 1989), 24ff. Loder on C.S. Lewis, 131ff. On Loder's use of Kierkegaard see Kenneth E. Kovacs, *The Relational Theology of James E. Loder: Encounter and Conviction* (New York: Peter Lang, 2011).

often neglected aspect of the Christian life: Christ's reign over our lives, Christ's reign over the world. A text such as Colossians 1 lifts up a particular image of Christ and the Church and the world, of the world that is to come, but also the world as it already now is by God's grace. And Colossians 1, especially verses 15-20, is crammed with Christological significance—we could be here all day, all week, indeed a lifetime, unpacking what Paul is claiming here in this text that was probably written as a hymn to Christ.

The honest question before us is this: is this text imaginary or imaginative? Is it just wishful thinking, a fancy of what the world might be? Perhaps. Or is it a baptized imaginative rendering of reality rooted in the person and work of Christ, what he accomplished, what he continues to offer the world?[3] Colossians casts a vision here for us, and it's up to you and me to decide: imaginary or imaginative?

Paul's answer is pretty clear. It's imaginative. In fact, either Paul or the writer of this hymn wants us to pay attention to the *image* that shapes our *imagination*. For the hymn says Christ was the "image of the invisible God" (Col. 1:15). The Greek here is *ikon*. We could also translate it as "symbol." Christ is the *ikon*, the symbol, the image of the invisible God. It's important to remember that Paul understood an *ikon* or symbol as sharing in the reality it represents. That's what a symbol does, it participates in the reality toward which it points. A sign, by contrast, refers to itself, indicating a way or sharing a message (such as a Stop sign). A cross is a symbol, not a sign, because it represents, points to, and participates in a whole reality that stands behind it. Christ as *ikon* makes the invisible visible. He represents that deeper reality, the deeper truth, even as he participates in it.

Christ, therefore, is a manifestation of something else because as *ikon* he participates in a deeper reality, and that deeper reality is God. We see *through* him and see God. We see *through* him and discover God's intention for the world. We see *through* him and discover God's plan of redemption and resurrection in the heart of all things. We see *through* him and discover that God's intention in Christ, as it was from the beginning of time, is to reconcile *all things* through Christ and in Christ.

All things—*ta panta*, in Greek—every order of the universe, every level of reality, every principality, power, authority, throne, and dominion. From the micro to the macro level, the work of Christ on the cross was to reconcile, to make peace with and among all the powers of the world, in order that every principality and power and throne and dominion might yield its authority and serve the benevolent intentions of God. Christ's life and ministry and

---

[3] The notion of the imagination baptized is taken from Lewis in *Surprised by Joy: The Shape of My Early Life* (New York: Harvest/HBJ, 1955), 181.

resurrection together mark the "beginning" of this work, and his life and ministry, resurrection and ascension show us that it's God's desire to fill "all things" with Christ's presence. To fill all things. To dwell among us. To fill every aspect of our lives with God's presence. Christ sums up God's intention for the entire cosmos: to fill all things. There is nothing and no one outside the scope of Christ's presence and power. That's the goal. That's also the claim for reality, right now, because of the resurrection.

Now, you can say all of this is imaginary theological mumbo-jumbo, a flight of fancy. Perhaps. Or maybe it's a baptized imaginative recasting of the world that, even now, the Spirit is crafting in order for us to see and feel and know that right now this new world is both here *and* on the way. This imaginative rendering of reality put Paul and the early church more deeply into the world, engaged with the world. It sent Paul traveling all over his world. They all knew that reality was different because of Christ. Indeed, reality is never the same when one is in Christ. We come to see that all things are held in Christ, and when we know this, trust this, indwell this truth, then everything changes. That's why Christ is the beginning of all things, the *arche* (Col. 1:18), and in him all things become new.

Paul lived in a world transfigured by the presence of Christ. And Paul extends that invitation to us, to see the world from that perspective, to see ourselves as already participating in the power and presence of Christ, to be *en Christos*, in Christ, as Paul loved to say, to exist in Christ.

And this is the claim of the early Church: to be in Christ means that we exist in the midst of the Christ who has *already* reconciled us to God, who has *already* reconciled every wayward power and principality in the universe. Not someday. Not one day. Right now, we are reconciled. We live in a world that is no longer at enmity with God. Right now. In him all things hold together.

Now, you're probably thinking that I'm completely detached from reality, that this is an imaginary flight of fancy. This isn't the way the world is. This is ludicrous. Perhaps. Or maybe this is an imaginative rendering of the world as it is and is becoming. It's a rendering of reality in the light of Christ that helps us to see what the world was created for, through which we understand the meaning of Christ's life, a rendering of reality that helps us to discern the shape and scope and meaning of our lives. Through this imaginative rendering, we realize that we are not where we will be, and so we begin again the process of waiting and hoping for Christ to be born yet again into our lives, so that our lives and the life of the world might conform to that image, that *ikon*, that vision we find in Christ.

That's the goal, which is already here and on the way. I'm not making this up. It's how Paul describes the Christian life. It's the imaginative vision that transfigures the here and now; we are on the way to becoming what is already true. Now and then.

I know, it all sounds abstract. Perhaps C.S. Lewis is helpful here. This is what he wants us to imagine, imaginations baptized, to see what Christ has done and is doing in us, through us, for us. Lewis wrote:

> Imagine yourself as a living house. God comes in to rebuild that house. At first, perhaps, you can understand what [God] is doing. [God] is getting the drains right and stopping the leaks in the roof and so on; you knew that those jobs needed doing and so you are not surprised. But presently [God] starts knocking the house about in a way that hurts abominably and does not seem to make any sense. What on earth is [God] up to? The explanation is that [God] is building quite a different house from the one you thought of—throwing out a new wing here, putting on an extra floor there, running up towers, making courtyards. You thought you were being made into a decent little cottage: but [God] is building a palace. [God] intends to come and live in it Himself.[4]

Our lives a *palace*—expansive and large. For "Once a King [once a Queen] in Narnia, always a King [always a Queen]."[5] And so the work continues. For truly God intends to come and live in us.

---

[4] C.S. Lewis, *Mere Christianity* (New York: Macmillan, 1960), 174. Lewis borrowed this analogy from George MacDonald (1824-1905).
[5] C.S. Lewis, *The Lion, the Witch, and the Wardrobe* (New York: Collier Books, 1970), 186.

Sounding Through:
On Pastoral Identity

On the 23rd of September 1990, at the First Presbyterian Church of North Arlington, NJ, I was ordained Minister of Word & Sacrament. I answered the Constitutional questions and then knelt for the laying on hands, which took place several feet away from the font where I had been baptized twenty-six years earlier. As I approach the anniversary of my ordination, I've been thinking a lot about what it means to be a pastor. And so I was grateful for Adam Walker Cleveland's invitation to contribute something to this series on pastoral identity.

After twenty-five years of ministry in three very different congregations, I'm still trying to figure what it means to be a pastor. What I have come to know, at least, is this: my pastoral identity is grounded in my baptismal identity, and who I am as a child of God is related to my life as a pastor, but they are not the same. I'm grateful that I was ordained where I was baptized. One led to the other, one informs and shapes the other, but they're not the same. Remembering my baptism grounds me in who I am; it reminds me who I am, *first*, as a person, as a child of God, and then, *second*, as a pastor. It's out of my baptismal identity that I find I'm being called, again and again, to serve God's people in particular ways.

Indwelling the connection between baptism and ordination, I've come to see that God's call is to *all* of me and not just part of me. This relatively recent insight arrived after many years of internal struggle. All of me was and is claimed in the waters of my baptism. Therefore, God's call is directed toward me, to all of me—not part of me, not just the "churchy" part, or the part that had perfect church school attendance, or the Master of Divinity part, or the PresbyGeek part, not just the "religious" or "Christian" or "spiritual part" of me. God summons all of me, the totality of my being, both spirit and body, both who I think I am, consciously, *as well as the part of me that is unconscious,* unknown to me but known to God.

Why is this so important? *Because in ministry it's so easy to lose one's soul.* It's so easy to lose one's self, forget one's self—and not in a good way. And one of the fastest and easiest ways to lose one's soul is by taking on the expectations and role projections of both congregation and society.

It's easy for pastors to conflate their self-identities with the image/prestige/influence of the congregations that they serve. Some begin to think they are their congregations, which is disastrous for ministry—both for the minister and for the church. This is how you lose your soul.

It's easy for pastors to meld their personal self-identities with their public roles or personas. Then they begin to believe they are their personas, which is disastrous and destructive—both for a minister and for a congregation. This, too, is how you lose your soul.

We all have personas. They're necessary, important. They help us navigate through the world. Our pastoral personas are equally necessary, essential, and remarkably useful. And, yet, I've come to know that while my pastoral persona is how I appear to the world, as well as to myself, it doesn't exhaust who I am, the core of my being "hidden with Christ in God" (Col. 3:3).

It was C. G. Jung (1875-1961) who spoke about persona from a psychoanalytic perspective. Persona "originally meant the mask worn by an actor, signifying the role [s/he] played".[1] As such, Jung explains, "the persona is nothing real: it is a compromise between the individual and society as to what [one] should be. [S/he] takes a name, earns a title, represents an office, is this or that. In a certain sense all this is real, yet in relation to the *essential individuality of the person concerned* it is only a secondary reality, a product of compromise, in making which others often have a greater share then [s/he.]"[2] The persona is a particular mask, chosen by the ego to hide from or cover something else, which enables an actor to perform. In extreme cases the persona can be completely at odds with one's soul, which can lead to vocational crises and psychological breakdowns. For most, there is always something of one's core identity reflected in one's persona. Our personas are *personal*, which prevent us from becoming complete shams, and yet the persona is not to be confused with one's soul or core self.

Jung reminds us that "the Latin *persona* came from *per sonare*, to sound through, because masks had a sort of tube inside, from the actor's mouth into the mouth of the mask, a built-in megaphone to amplify the sound so it would carry."[3]

I love this image. *To sound through.*

We all need a pastoral persona, a kind of mask unique to each person, that allows our core self, our individualities, all that we have come to know

---

[1] C. G. Jung, "The Relations Between the Ego and the Unconscious" *The Collected Works of C. G. Jung.* Vol. 7 (Princeton: Princeton University Press, 1977), §245.
[2] Jung, *CW* 7, §246. Emphasis added.
[3] William McGuire and R. F. C. Hull, eds. *C. G. Jung Speaking: Interviews & Encounters* (Princeton: Princeton University Press, 1993), 210.

personally of God's grace and goodness in Christ, to sound through. But our pastoral personas must not be confused with what is trying to sound through us.

Because I don't believe the Spirit called me to live out a persona, I try to live from the deepest core of who I am, grounded in my baptismal identity, and then try to let this core self sound through me, thus bringing my experience to bear upon how I live out my call. Who I am is deeper than my pastoral persona; therefore, I try to wear this mask lightly.

I often draw strength from Dietrich Bonhoeffer's (1906-1945) deeply personal, brutally honest poem, WHO AM I? included among his *Letters and Papers from Prison*. In this piece we're privy to hear a conversation he's having with himself as he tries to reclaim his soul, as it were, out from under his pastoral identity or role. As a prisoner of the Third Reich in Tegel prison in Berlin, awaiting execution, Bonhoeffer ministered to his fellow prisoners. They became his congregation. Here in this piece, from July 1944, we find a seasoned pastor wrestling with who he is.

> Who am I? They often tell me
> I would step from my cell's confinement
> calmly, cheerfully, firmly,
> like a squire from his country-house.
>
> Who am I? They often tell me
> I would talk to my warders
> freely and friendly and clearly,
> as though it were mine to command.
>
> Who am I? They also tell me
> I would bear the days of misfortune
> equably, smilingly, proudly,
> like one accustomed to win.
>
> Am I then really all that which other men tell of?
> Or am I only what I know of myself,
> restless and longing and sick, like a bird in a cage,
> struggling for breath, as though hands were compressing my throat,
> yearning for colors, for flowers, for the voices of the birds,
> thirsting for words of kindness, for neighborliness,
> trembling with anger at despotisms and petty humiliation,
> tossing in expectation of great events,
> powerlessly trembling for friends at an infinite distance,
> weary and empty at praying, at thinking, at making,
> faint, and ready to say farewell to it all?

Who am I? This or the other?
Am I one person today, and tomorrow another?
Am I both at once? A hypocrite before others,
and before myself a contemptibly woebegone weakling?
Or is something within me still like a beaten army,
fleeing in disorder from victory already achieved?

Who am I? They mock me, these lonely questions of mine.
Whoever I am, thou knowest, O God, I am thine.[4]

This essay was included in a blog series on pastoral identity for POMOMUSINGS, hosted by Adam Walker Cleveland, March 16, 2015.
http://pomomusings.com/2015/03/16/ken-kovacs-on-pastoral-identity-sounding-through/.

---

[4] Dietrich Bonhoeffer, *Letters & Papers from Prison*, Eberhard Bethge, ed. New York: Macmillan, 1972.

Containing the Sacred

[Dogma] ... ritual ... cultic practices ... these artifacts of primal experience in time become institutions, and progressively more and more remote from the original encounter with the gods. We all know this is true. If these institutional forms really connected people with the gods, we could see the difference.[1]

I remember the exact moment I read these words ten years ago. It was an experience of resonance and recognition. With considerable excitement I wrote in the margin, in red ink, *Yes! Yes!*

These words have become a constant companion, informing my journey and vocation, and, at times, showing up in dreams. They mirrored back to me what I've been feeling for some time, but could not articulate. It was James Hollis who did this for me. I was unfamiliar with his work at that time. I remember wandering one day through Politics & Prose, one of my favorite bookstores in Washington, DC, when my eye was drawn to this title: *Creating a Life: Finding Your Individual Path*. I devoured the book (or, better, it devoured me). This was my first introduction to the searching insight and wisdom that one consistently finds in Hollis. Reading this text also signaled my return to the thought of C. G. Jung, which I first encountered as a religion and history major at Rutgers College.

Hollis is right. If religious institutions were doing a good job helping people connect with the gods, we would see the difference. This applies to all religions, of course. But as a life-long Presbyterian and a minister in the Presbyterian Church (USA) for more than twenty-four years, I read Hollis, through the filter of my own experience, as a veiled yet honest and accurate critique of the contemporary Church, particularly in Europe and North America. If the Church was really doing a good job helping individuals connect with God, the *numinosum*, we would be seeing the difference. It would be evident. But it's not.

The Church is in trouble. Christianity is in trouble. These are overly generalized statements, to be sure. Of course there are many churches led by dedicated and gifted clergy who are passionately and imaginatively engaged in helping people connect with the Holy. It is happening and making a difference in those locations. And there are even some clergy who are optimistic about the current state of the Church. It's obvious that the Church these days is undergoing a massive transition or reformation, the kind that

---

[1] James Hollis, *Creating a Life: Finding Your Individual Path* (Toronto: Inner City Books, 2001), 57

seems to occur once every 500 years.² I suspect, though, that something deeper is going on.

As I talk with colleagues and friends, especially those working in denominational offices, they are less than positive about the prospects of the Church. Congregations are struggling with massive membership decline, the financial burden of caring for aging buildings (many of which were built after World War II when it was "American" to go to church), sexual and financial scandals, eroding trust in authority (especially institutional authority), the polarizing liberal-conservative political rhetoric infecting worshipping communities, all of which contribute to a crisis of identity for the Church. People are moving away from Christianity because of what they see going on in the Church. This is not to say that people no longer have a desire for the Holy or no longer have religious experiences, because they do. People are moving away from the Church because very often (not always, but often) it fails to speak to the deep, human desire to connect with the Holy, to something numinous. These direct encounters with Mystery are occurring apart from the ministrations of religious institutions. "Is it not a paradox," Hollis asks in his recent work, *Hauntings*, "that the chief practical function of so many religious organizations is to protect people from religious experience? Are they afraid that the faithful might go off the reservation?"³

People have left and continue to leave the "reservation," in droves. And many are being drawn to Jung precisely because they appreciate his "spiritual" or "mystical" vision and because he seems to stand outside conventional religious traditions, particularly Christianity. Some have even argued that Jung was trying to create a new religion as an alternative to Christianity and the teachings of the Church. There is much in Jung that could and does provide a sanctuary for disenchanted Church-goers, those who wish to be "spiritual" but not religious, apart from religious institutions.

However, the more I read Jung—Jung, not necessarily Jungians—it's difficult to subscribe to the notion that he was trying to form a new religion. Neither do I feel that his theories are always incompatible with orthodox Christianity, although it's certainly easy to think so. *Memories, Dreams, Reflections* offers many examples of his disappointment with the faith of his father, a Reformed Church pastor. Jung's blistering critique of the Church throughout his writings, his frustration with theologians who accuse him of "psychologizing" the Gospel, and his own "theological," seemingly heretical

---

² See Phyllis Trickle, *The Great Emergence: How Christianity is Changing and Why* (Baker Books, 2012).
³ James Hollis, *Hauntings: Dispelling the Ghosts Who Run Our Lives* (Ashville, NC: Chiron Publications, 2013), 25.

writings over the last third of his life, could effortlessly lead one to conclude that Jung was against the Church and that he wasn't a Christian.

Yet, it's significant that Sonu Shamdasani firmly places Jung within the Christian tradition. In the 1930s, Jung said that he stood on the extreme left wing of Protestantism.[4] And even though, as Shamdasani concedes, the *Red Book* (*Liber Novus*) "*is* a heretical text ... it remains within a Christian framework."[5] In a conversation with James Hillman, Shamdasani makes this remarkable observation: "If there were an index [to the *Red Book*], it would show that the critical figure is Christ. In Jung's later writings, [he claimed that] the development of the Christian tradition led to a suppression of what he calls individual symbol formation, so that it had blocked access to direct religious experience. This was what he saw his whole endeavor as recovering."[6] This was not only Jung's "endeavor" in the *Red Book*, but throughout his life's *opus*. "In Jung's view," Shamdasani suggests, "recovering the full depth and range of individual symbol formation is the way forward, paradoxically, to the revivification of Christianity."[7] As a Protestant, Jung knew what was lost in Protestantism, "individual symbol formation." Indeed, in a striking comment, Shamdasani insists that Jung was not against the Church, but that, on the contrary, the "task [Jung] takes up [in the *Red Book*] is one of revivifying ecclesiastical Christianity."[8]

What I increasingly hear in Jung is the voice of a prophet seeking the reform of the Church. As a prophet Jung is severely critical of the Church; however, like all prophets, he sees things that others cannot see (or refuse to see): he sees its untapped potential. Jung has a vision for what the Church could be and the invaluable service it could provide, not only to Christians and Christianity, but also to a larger society, when a community of people (a real *koinonia*) risks serious intimacy with the wisdom of the psyche. Jung wrote that the "dogmatically formulated truths of the Christian Church express, almost perfectly, the nature of psychic experience. They are the repositories of the secrets of the soul, and this matchless knowledge is set forth in grand symbolical images. The unconscious thus possesses a natural affinity with the spiritual values of the Church, particularly in their dogmatic form, which owes its special character to centuries of theological controversy...and to the passionate efforts of many great men." Jung continues, "The Church would

---

[4] C. G. Jung, "The Relation of Psychotherapy to the Cure of Souls," *The Collected Works of C. G. Jung*, (Princeton: Princeton University Press, 1977) §537. See also James Hillman & Sonu Shamdasani, *Lament of the Dead: Psychology after Jung's* Red Book (New York: W. W. Norton & Co, 2013), 123.
[5] Hillman & Shamdasani, 117.
[6] Hillman & Shamdasani, 117-118.
[7] Hillman & Shamdasani, 119.
[8] Hillman & Shamdasani, 124.

be an ideal solution for anyone seeking a suitable receptacle for the chaos of the unconscious were it not that everything man-made, however refined, has its imperfections."[9] It's difficult for the Church to be a container for the psyche when it's rent asunder by centuries of division and dissension.

The challenges facing the Church today are enormous, but I haven't given up on it—thanks to Jung. Indeed, what if the Church really saw itself as a *vas temenos*—not a sacred container, but a container of the sacred, the "secrets of the soul"? Instead of the Church conflating itself with its contents, its sacred "secrets," what if the Church really saw itself *in service to* the sacred and viewed itself as the *conduit*, the means, and the place where a connection with the Holy might actually occur, a community that helps individuals live into the transformation that inevitably occurs when one encounters the Holy? It would be a Church that values, celebrates, welcomes, and facilitates these kinds of connections, providing a "safe" place for individuals to have direct, primal religious experiences—a relatively safe place, that is. For what encounter with the Holy or *numinosum* is ever entirely safe? Just imagine: if more of the Church took this approach to its mission, we would definitely see the difference.

This essay was originally titled "How Jung Led Me ~~Away From~~ Toward Christianity," published in the C. G. Jung Society of Atlanta Newsletter, November 2014.

---

[9] C. G. Jung, "The Psychology of Transference," *The Collected Works of C. G. Jung*, Vol. 16 (Princeton: Princeton University Press, 1977), §391.

The Eyes of Experience: A Theological Essay on Job 42:1-6[1]

And Job answered Yahweh:

> "I know that you can do all things, and that no purpose of yours
>   can be thwarted.
> *'Who is this that hides counsel without knowledge?'*
> Therefore, I have uttered what I did not understand,
>   things too wonderful for me, which I did not know.
> *'Hear, and I will speak; I will question you, and you declare to me.'*
> I had heard of you by the hearing of the ear,
>   but now my eye sees you;
> therefore, I despise myself, and repent in dust and ashes."
>
> Job 42:1-6

I wish scribes had etched in the text of Job, right at the start of Chapter 42, in big, bold letters: STOP: *SILENCE*. It's been said, often by mystics, that all wisdom begins and ends in silence. One needs to be silent long enough for wisdom to emerge. And the Book of Job is all about wisdom, a particular kind of wisdom, which means that engaging it requires silence.

The Book of Job is one of the most challenging books in the Bible. Along with Ecclesiastes, Song of Songs, Psalms, Proverbs, Wisdom, and Sirach, the Book of Job belongs to the genre of scripture known as wisdom literature.[2] Originally ascribed to Moses, its author is unknown. It was written somewhere between the seventh and fourth centuries before the Common Era, most likely in the sixth century BCE, when Israel was in exile in Babylon. It's often assumed that the story is trying to address the theodicy question: Why do the righteous or innocent suffer? A thorough reading of the text, however, suggests that the narrative never really gives a convincing answer to this question. Scholars suspect that the Book of Job was included in the biblical canon in response to inadequate theological claims found in Deuteronomy, namely that blessing comes only by following God's Law, that is, that blessing is a reward for remaining faithful to the covenant with

---

[1] This essay, written for The Zurich Laboratory (April 2015), conforms to Modern Language Association (MLA) formatting and style. http://www.zurichlab.org/#!research-articles/c6sb.

[2] Wisdom and Sirach are deuterocanonical texts placed in the Apocrypha by Protestant Bible translators.

Yahweh.³ The author of Job knows that things are not that simple, that life, especially life with Yahweh, is infinitely more complex.

Here's an overview of the story. In the opening verses, we read: "There was once a man in the land of Uz whose name was Job. That man was blameless and upright, one who feared God and turned away from evil" (1:1). Job is described as a wealthy man, with seven sons, three daughters, and a beloved wife. The story's attention then shifts to the court of heaven, where "heavenly beings," including Satan—Satan is understood here to be a member of Yahweh's court, not the personification of evil—present themselves before the throne.⁴ Satan questions Job's piety, suggesting that Job's devotion to Yahweh is conditional, that he worships Yahweh only because of Yahweh's blessings. Yahweh agrees to Satan's plan to test Job. And so Job's wealth and children are removed. Job responds: "Naked I came from my mother's womb, and naked shall I return there: Yahweh gave, and Yahweh has taken away; blessed be the name of the Yahweh" (1:21). Satan continues to torment Job further, inflicting him with painful sores and boils on his skin such that he sits among the ashes in mourning. Job refuses to give up on Yahweh.

Three friends arrive—Eliphas, Bildad, and Zophar—to talk with Job, to help him make sense of his suffering, to search for meaning. They believe that Job's suffering is a punishment for sin. But how can this be, since Job is "blameless and upright"? Still, Job struggles with what's happening to him. He searches for wisdom in the midst of his suffering and finds little. At a moment of extreme frustration, he says, "I loathe my life; I will give free utterance to my complaint; I will speak in the bitterness of my soul" (10:1). And so he directs his complaint toward Yahweh: "Why did you bring me from the womb? Would that I had died before any eye had seen me, and were as though I had not been, carried from the womb to the grave. Are not the days of my life few? Let me alone, that I may find a little comfort before I go, never to return, to the land of gloom and deep darkness, the land of gloom and chaos, where light is like darkness" (10:18-22).

Job's suffering and frustration deepen. "My skin turns black and falls from me, and my bones burn with heat. My lyre is turned to mourning, and my pipe to the voice of those who weep" (20:30-31). Job makes one more declaration of his innocence before he is silenced. The three "friends" go away, and a new voice begins to speak. It is Elihu, who rebukes Job and

---

³ For an in-depth exploration of theological themes and historical contexts in the Book of Job, see Franzen. Both the Hebrew and Christian testaments are dialogical in nature: they answer, respond to, react to, and redact the multiple traditions and sources of which they are made.

⁴ It is significant to note that in Job, Satan is a member of the court of Yahweh, not the personification of evil; the latter portrayal develops later within Judaism. In Job, Satan is on God's payroll, as it were. *Ha-Satan* in Hebrew means "the adversary" or "the accuser."

explains to him that only the kind of wisdom that comes from God is sufficient for the sufferings and burdens of life. "For God speaks in one way, and in two, though people do not perceive it. In a dream, in a vision of the night, when deep sleep falls on mortals, while they slumber on their beds, then he opens their ears." (33:14-15).

And then, finally, Yahweh answers Job out of the whirlwind: "Who is this that darkens counsel by words without knowledge? Gird up your loins like a man, I will question you, and you shall declare to me. Where were you when I laid the foundation of the earth? Tell me." (38:2-4). Then, on and on, Yahweh speaks in these wild sermons out of the whirlwind, Chapters 38 through 41. Yahweh responds to Job's unyielding demand for an explanation for his suffering. Yahweh cross-examines Job with question after question. The Voice shakes Job's foundation, shatters everything he assumes and believes—about himself, his neighbors, his precarious hold on reality, his place in the universe, even his image of the God. On and on and on, Yahweh graciously assaults the old man's sensibilities and reason, questions everything Job thought he knew about everything. Then, at the end of Chapter 41, Yahweh stops speaking.

And it's precisely here, I suggest, that silence is called for. Instead, the Bible offers a seamless transition from Chapter 41 to these extraordinary verses in Chapter 42, when Job answers Yahweh. Let's hear these verses again, this time using Stephen Mitchell's poetic translation of the text:

> Then Job said to the Unnamable:
> I know you can do all things
> and nothing you wish is impossible.
> *Who is this whose ignorant words*
>   *cover my design with darkness?*
> I have spoken of the unspeakable and tried to grasp the infinite.
>   *Listen and I will speak;*
>   *I will question you: please, instruct me.*
> I had heard of you with my ears; but now my eyes have seen you.
>   Therefore, I will be quiet, comforted that I am dust. (88)

Now, there's a lot going on in these six verses. It's essential that we follow the flow of this exchange between Job and Yahweh and between Job and himself.

Again, it's here, in this liminal space between Chapters 41 and 42, that we need to create space for silence: *hold your tongue, hush, listen, behold*. At this point I imagine Job speechless, breathless, gasping for air, traumatized, in shock. Before him, from out of the whirlwind, is the Voice of the Unnamable, the

Holy One, this *mysterium tremendum et fascinans*, this mystery that fascinates even as it overwhelms.[5]

Imagine yourself in Job's skin. Put yourself in his experience. Imagine what his encounter with Yahweh must have felt like for him. What does one say in such a moment? What does one say in a moment of being totally overwhelmed, the kind that leaves you speechless? What do you say when you're completely overcome by life or reality, struck by beauty or tragedy (perhaps both at the same time)? How do you respond? What is there to say? Often there's nothing to say. Language is inadequate. And so we are brought to silence.

Then, from out of the silence, with humbled conviction born of experience, Job begins to speak. And it's precisely here, I think, that we find the theological nerve center of the Book of Job. Job's answer to Yahweh, his response here, is wild and electric like the voice of God. Job acknowledges, "I know you can do all things and nothing you wish is impossible." Then Job recalls the question Yahweh first poses to him from out of the whirlwind. But now Job turns the question toward *himself* and asks: "Who is this whose ignorant words cover my design with darkness?"[6] Who, indeed? Who is this God? Wrestling with the truth now unfolding before him, Job confesses this stunning insight: "I have spoken of the unspeakable and tried to grasp the infinite."

Job then recalls other words from Yahweh, when Yahweh sarcastically chastised him for his arrogant complaints: "Listen and I will speak: I will question *you*, please, instruct me."[7]

Finally, Job comes to the moment of revelation, a moment of life-changing insight. In profound realization, he says, "I had heard of you with my ears; but now my eyes have seen you. Therefore, I will be quiet, comforted that I am dust."

From silence to silence.

It's easy to overlook the significance of Job's confession here. Many turn to Job searching for reasons why the innocent suffer. As stated earlier, the text never really provides a convincing response to the theodicy question. But there's another way to read the text.

---

[5] It is significant to note that in the Book of Job, Satan is a member of the court of Yahweh, not the personification of evil; the latter portrayal develops later within Judaism. In Job, Satan is on God's payroll, as it were. *Ha-Satan* in Hebrew means "the adversary" or "the accuser."
[6] This is originally asked of Job in 38.2.
[7] This is originally directed at Job in 40.7; emphasis is mine.

Centuries ago, it was William Blake (1757-1827) who proposed a different interpretive lens worthy of consideration. Blake spent an enormous amount of time immersed in Job's story, eventually producing twenty-two marvelous engravings illustrating it through his singular theological lens. For Blake, the Book of Job is less about why the innocent suffer than it is about personal *transformation*.[8] It's about *metanoia*, the change of mind that occurs when we come to the limits of our knowing and find ourselves confronted by the face of the living God.

You see, prior to the whirlwind, Job's moral universe is clearly intact, consisting of well-defined distinctions between right and wrong. When the Book of Job was written, it was assumed that individuals received either reward or punishment for their actions. God was understood to be the judge. "Job's [initial] case against God assumes not that the [judicial] system is wrong ... but that God has failed to govern the created order justly." In other words, Job questions God's justice.[9] Job is subsequently questioned by God, however, and soon discovers that the system is not what he thought it was, that there's more going on around him than meets the eye. This is what Jungian analyst James Hollis refers to as "the collapse of our tacit contract with the universe—the assumption that if we act correctly, if we are of good heart and good intentions, things will work out. We assume a reciprocity with the universe. If we do our part, the universe will comply. Many ancient stories, including the Book of Job, painfully reveal the fact that there is no such contract." To discover this is one of the "most powerful shocks" we can experience.[10]

Exhausted, desperate, Job hits a theological wall. He discovers that the religious views of his community—all the things he learned in "Sabbath school"—are not equal to the existential challenge of facing Yahweh, the apparent injustices in the world, and the complexities of reality. In other words, Job's theological worldview is insufficient to the task before him. He cannot speak to the complexity of his experience, this man who has been to hell and back, who has looked into the face of the void, having lost family, friends, the flesh on his bones. This man, full of sores and grieving in ashes, asks, *Why? Why?* Job's trauma calls into question *everything*. He arrives at a point where his understanding of God (that is, his image of God or God-image) can no longer yield sufficient meaning in the face of horrific tragedy. While Job never gives up on God—at one point his wife tells him just to "curse God, and die" (Job 2:9)—in the end, Job discovers that he has to give

---

[8] *Illustrations of the Book of Job* was completed in 1825 and published in 1826. See Raine and Edinger.
[9] See Hester.
[10] Hollis suggests that this discovery often takes place during one's middle years, the so-called "Middle Passage."

up his old understanding of God and God's justice in order to experience something radically new. What's more, he cannot experience this on his own. He becomes capable of it only when he comes up against his limits.

At one point (or many), we all hit a similar wall when we realize that our perspectives are too narrow and limited and we're called (or sometimes forced) to yield to a wider frame of knowing. In his essay *A Defense of Poetry*, written in 1821, poet Percy Bysshe Shelley (1792-1822) said that poetry "purg[es] the film of familiarity which obscures from us the wonder of our being."[11] Something of the same is required in order for us to "see" God. The "film of familiarity" is wiped away and we're allowed to see something anew. Job confronts the inadequacy of his former ways of framing the world. His new experience yields a wider, more comprehensive view of reality, of justice, even of God. It's a gracious reframing of his world, his self, the God he thought he knew—something far more profound and expansive. Job's vision changes everything.

I believe similar visions do occur, not necessarily in the literal sense (although I'm sure that's possible), but in varieties of experience that yield a similar reframing of existence. I'm using *seeing* here as a metaphor for transformed perception. I'm talking about a moment or many moments over the course of a lifetime—moments of extraordinary insight, encounters with the numinous, religious experiences of significant power and terror and even beauty—when the Holy helps us "see" what we could not "see" before, giving us new "spectacles," as John Calvin (1509-1564) liked to say (135), allowing us to see more clearly in the "theatre" of God's glory.

To see. That's the critical point.[12] Says Job: "I had heard of you with my ears"—that is, before— "but now my eyes see you." *My eyes. My experience.* Wisdom received through my perception, not someone else's. More than hearing *about* God, Job comes to know God for himself firsthand. And yet, significantly, what Job is able to discern, what he's able to perceive, comes to him only upon hearing the Voice from out of the whirlwind. Job's ability to see with fresh eyes is contingent upon what he *hears*. This should not be surprising given the value, within Israel's experience, placed on hearing. "Hear, O Israel, the LORD our God, the LORD is one" (Deuteronomy 6.4). Yahweh consistently summons people to hear. The divine Word speaks, and when heard, new worlds come into being. Lives are formed and reformed;

---

[11] Published posthumously by Edward Moxon in Essays, Letters from Abroad, Translations and Fragments (London, 1840). Cited in Paul Bishop, *Jung's Answer to Job: An Answer* (Brunner-Routledge, 2002), 50.
[12] The use of "seeing" may be problematic, particularly for those who are visually impaired. "Sight" is to be interpreted metaphorically (as perception, awareness, a way of coming to understanding) as well; a literal interpretation is not necessary.

perspectives are changed, transfigured; and we are given a new set of "eyes" to perceive ourselves, our neighbors, and the world.[13]

Job discovers the inadequacy of faith that comes through hearsay, the kind that is passed on from others and received passively. It's been said that "the person who hungers and thirsts after justice is not satisfied with a menu. It is not enough for [one] to hope or believe or know that there is absolute justice in the universe: [one] must taste and see it" (Mitchell xxvii). Surely Job has heard about God, about what God is like. He had lived secure in his understanding—that is, until everything falls apart. What he receives graciously in the end is not the inherited faith of tradition nor the pious platitudes of well-intentioned family and friends, but something far more valuable, something that comes through his own existential encounter—a journey only he can take, yielding wisdom learned not from afar nor at arm's length but within his guts, his heart. It is something of God that cannot be taught in a classroom or found in a book. It has to be *felt*.

Now, all of this might appear plainly obvious, not terribly significant or even radical. However, within the Reformed theological tradition (where I stand, theologically), giving too much weight to personal religious experience often makes us very uneasy.[14] Reformed Christians (and we are certainly not alone here) live with an ongoing tension between what is known through *revelation*—God's truth, wisdom, and grace come "down" from above, as it were—and *human experience*. Theologically speaking, it's a question of epistemology. How does one come to know what one knows? How does one come to know God, to trust in Christ, to experience grace?

Generally speaking, the Reformed tradition stresses that whatever we know of God comes to us because God chooses to reveal it to us directly. This knowledge does not emerge naturally, that is, by way of human reason or subjective experience. It is given, and we receive it. We don't move toward such knowledge; it's a gift. The Reformed tradition privileges God's revelation and is reluctant to put too much stock in the authority of human experience.[15] Implicit in this view is the belief that experience cannot always

---

[13] The early followers of Jesus of Nazareth viewed him as "the Word [become] flesh" who "lived among us, and we have seen his glory..." (John 1.14). The voice of Yahweh is heard in Jesus. Similarly, Christians are summoned to "listen to him." See Matthew 17.5.

[14] The Reformed theological tradition is a major branch of Protestantism generally associated with the thought and practice of John Calvin (1509-1564) in Geneva, Ulrich Zwingli (1484-1531) and Heinrich Bullinger (1504-1575) in Zürich, and John Knox (c. 1514-1572) in Edinburgh. Today, the heirs of this tradition are part of the World Alliance of Reformed Churches, which has 218 member churches, denominations in 107 countries around the world, and some 75 million members. http://wcrc.ch/

[15] In many respects, C. G. Jung's so-called gnostic bent, privileging personal experience or knowledge over the authority of tradition and religious institutions, helpfully exposes some of

be trusted because all of our faculties of discernment are "fallen," subject to error, "bound" by the power of sin, and therefore distorted and thus inadequate. And so the Reformed tradition prefers to build its theological systems on so-called "objective" ideas gathered from an authoritative text.

Trusting experience can be messy, complicated. How can it be verified? Substantiated? It's far too individualistic. And it's risky. Is divine revelation "finished" or "closed," or can there be new things to discover? Can human experience be a medium of revelation? If so, will there be wisdom or knowledge that emerges from personal experience that goes beyond or even supersedes what we find within the received Jewish and Christian traditions? These are enormous theological questions. Even the suggestion that new revelation is possible borders on heresy for some Christians.

Yet for all these concerns (and they need to be taken seriously), experience still has to count for something, doesn't it? We need to lift up something often forgotten in religious communities: experience of God is prior to dogmatic formulation. Indeed, experience grounds conviction. All that we know in our hearts; all that we know deep in our souls; all of our losses, our traumas, our sufferings, our relationships, our gifts, our personalities; what is both conscious and unconscious—all of these are caught up in the mix of what we know of God and how we know God. Augustine (354-430) asserts, "To know myself is to know you, O God."[16] Yes, theology isn't biography, but we can't disconnect the two that easily; we must not discount the value of human experience.

And yet, sadly, there are people both in and outside the Church who have been told not to trust their experiences. They've been taught to question the value of their feelings and experiences, to discount them. For example, I know there are countless people in the Church who have had profound religious experiences but never say a word about them. Why is this? And there are countless others who have had profound religious experiences and left the Church because they couldn't find a community that took them seriously. There are people who are hungry to share something of what they have learned through their encounters with God, experiences not that

---

the shortcomings of the Reformed outlook. I contend that Jung offers a necessary and needed critique of the Reformed tradition while remaining situated within the Reformed tradition. In this sense he is very Protestant and very Reformed: *Ecclesia reformata semper reformanda* (the Church reformed and always being reformed). Indeed, Jung claims to stand on the extreme left wing of Protestantism (*CW* 11.537). Sonu Shamdasani believes that Jung "sees what's been lost in Protestantism," namely "individual symbol formation" (*Lament for the Dead* 119).

[16] *Viderim me, viderim te*. Quoted by St. Teresa of Ávila (1515-1582) in *The Interior Castle, The Complete Works of St. Teresa*.

dissimilar to Job's. They want to be faithful to their experience, both individually as well as in community.

In one of her letters, Flannery O'Connor (1925-1964) wisely writes, "Conviction without experience makes for harshness" (97). We run the risk of becoming exceptionally harsh in emphasizing conviction and ignoring, if not silencing, the experiences of sisters and brothers who want to tell us something of God's transforming love.

I've found that far too many people fail to honor their experience. I have, regrettably and far too many times, discounted the value of mine. Instead, maybe, just maybe, we're called to value and *anticipate* an experience of God, even if doing so means refusing to fit it unquestioningly into traditional teachings. Even if it means opening ourselves "to new possibilities and surprises," as theologian David Ford suggests, "even in the sphere of [our] core convictions." And even if it means becoming people "who above all cry out with integrity before God and resist all attempts to misinterpret, marginalize, or stifle that cry" (129).

Such openness and integrity were especially true of the depth psychologist Carl Gustav Jung. His experience is especially relevant here, given that he came from a long line of Reformed pastors. Jung's father was a Swiss Reformed pastor near Basel, but Jung himself did not find any life in his father's faith. Jung was told that his First Communion would be a life-altering experience. Instead—nothing. "For me it was an absence of God and no religion," he said. "Church was a place to which I no longer could go. There was no life there, but death" (*Memories, Dreams, Reflections* 57). From an early age Jung had profound encounters with the Holy that forever changed the course of his life; even though they overwhelmed and scared him, he knew there was power to heal in them. They offered him hope, and he would spend the rest of his life trying to be faithful to them despite considerable resistance. They were, he said, moments of experience of a "direct living God"—the God that his father lacked and could not give to him. As Jung put it, "God alone was real—annihilating fire and an indescribable grace" (73). I love that. *Annihilating fire. Indescribable grace.*

In one of his last great works, *Mysterium Coniunctionis* (1955), Jung writes, "The experience of the Self is always a defeat for the ego" (546). While this might sound like a dogmatic assertion, the ground of this conviction was Jung's own personal encounter with what he described as the *Mysterium*, in 1913, just after his break with Sigmund Freud (1856-1939).[17]

What does Jung mean by Self? "The term 'Self,'" Edward F. Edinger (1922-1998) explains, "is used by Jung to designate a transpersonal center and totality of the psyche. It constitutes the greater objective personality, whereas the ego is the lesser, subjective personality. Empirically, the Self cannot be distinguished from the God-image. An encounter with it is a *mysterium tremendum*" (7). Ultimately it's this encounter with the Self or God-image, the *mysterium tremendum*, which transforms and transfigures Job's reality.[18]

Experiences of the Holy are not anomalies or signs of pathology. They should be anticipated. They are occurring all the time and need to be valued, honored, and respected within worshiping communities (maybe especially there) as well as in the consulting room of the psychoanalyst.[19]

In the end, Job's story says to us, *this* is what it's like to encounter the living God, to *know* God, not know *about* God. Not someone else's encounter, not someone else's story, not someone else's experience. Not a dead tradition but a living faith. It looks something like this: a life-changing, frame-bending experience of earthshattering significance, of radical insight, that comes over, around, in, through, and to us. An experience that opens our eyes—our eyes, not someone else's eyes, but ours—and allows us to see reality transfigured and transformed,[20] to see a new world, which despite all the pain and suffering and sorrow of our lives still has the capacity to yield meaning. It is an experience of the Living God that grounds all of our theological claims and creeds and epistemologies, that sets our hearts on fire and fires our imaginations, that sends us down new roads, wherever God wants to take us, following along with eyes that now can see.[21]

---

[17] The *Mysterium* encounter begins on December 21 and concludes on Christmas Day in 1913. Jung writes, "The mystery showed me in images what I should afterward live" (*The Red Book* 207).
[18] Edinger holds a similar understanding of the Book of Job, in that it "represents an individual ego's decisive encounter with the Self, the Greater Personality. The ego is wounded by this encounter which provokes a descent into the unconscious, a *neykia*. Because Job perseveres in questioning the meaning of the experience, his endurance is rewarded by a divine revelation. The ego, by holding fast to its integrity, is granted a realization of the Self" (11).
[19] I explore these ideas in "How Jung Led Me ~~Away From~~ Toward Christianity," C. G. Jung Society of Atlanta Newsletter, November 2014.
[20] See Loder and Kovacs' *The Relational Theology of James E. Loder: Encounter and Conviction*.
[21] I'm alluding here to the healing of the blind man Bartimaeus, a passage found in Mark 10.46-52, which could be a companion text to the Job reading. "Jesus and his disciples went to Jericho. And as they were leaving, they were followed by a large crowd. A blind beggar by the name of Bartimaeus son of Timaeus was sitting beside the road. When he heard that it was Jesus from Nazareth, he shouted, 'Jesus, Son of David, have pity on me!' Many people told

Holy One, give us more to see; give us ever more to see.

This has become my prayer.

---

the man to stop, but he shouted even louder, 'Son of David, have pity on me!' Jesus stopped and said, 'Call him over!' They called out to the blind man and said, 'Don't be afraid! Come on! He is calling for you.' The man threw off his coat as he jumped up and ran to Jesus. Jesus asked, 'What do you want me to do for you?' The blind man answered, 'Master, I want to see!' Jesus told him, 'You may go. Your eyes are healed because of your faith.' Right away the man could see, and he went down the road with Jesus." (*Contemporary English Version*)

References

Bouswma, William J. *John Calvin: A Sixteenth Century Portrait*. New York: OUP, 1988.

Edinger, Edward F. *Encounter with the Self: A Jungian Commentary on William Blake's* Illustrations of the Book of Job. Toronto: Inner City Books, 1983.

Ford, David. *Christian Wisdom: Desiring God and Learning in Love*. Cambridge: Cambridge UP, 2008.

Franzen, J. Gerald. *Job*. Atlanta: John Knox Press, 1985.

Hester, David C. *Job*. Louisville: Westminster John Knox Press, 2005.

Hillman, James and Sonu Shamdasani. *Lament of the Dead: Psychology after Jung's Red Book*. New York: W. W. Norton & Company, 2013.

Hollis, James. *The Middle Passage: From Misery to Meaning in Midlife*. Toronto: Inner City Books, 1993.

Huskinson, Lucy. "Holy, Holy, Holy: The Misappropriation of the Numinous in Jung." *The Idea of the Numinous: Contemporary Jungian and Psychoanalytic Perspectives*. Ed. Ann Casement and David Tacey. London: Routledge, 2006.

Jung, C. G. *Memories, Dreams, Reflections*. Ed. and recorded by Aniela Jaffé. Trans. Richard and Clara Winston. New York: Vintage Books, 1973.

———. *Mysterium Coiunctionis*, The Collected Works of C. G. Jung, Vol. 14. Princeton: Princeton UP, 1976.

———. "Psychotherapists or the Clergy," *The Collected Works of C. G. Jung*. Volume 11:488-538, Princeton: PUP, 1977.

———. *The Red Book* (Liber Novus). Ed. Sonu Shamdasani. Preface by Ulrich Hoerni. Trans. Mark Kyburz, John Peck, Sonu Shamdasani. New York: W.W. Norton & Co., 2009.

Kovacs, Kenneth E. "How Jung Led Me ~~Away From~~ Toward Christianity." In *C. G. Jung Society of Atlanta Newsletter*, November 2014.

———. *The Relational Theology of James E. Loder: Encounter and Conviction*. New York: Peter Lang, 2011.

Loder, James E. *The Transforming Moment*. 2nd ed. Colorado Springs, CO: Helmers & Howard, 1989.

O'Connor, Flannery. *The Habit of Being: Letters of Flannery O'Connor*. Selected and ed. Sally Fitzgerald. New York: Farrar, Strauss & Giroux, 1995.

Otto, Rudolph. *The Idea of the Holy: An Inquiry into the Non-Rational Factor in the Idea of the Divine and Its Relation to the Rational*. Trans. John H. Harvey. London: OUP, 1958.

Raine, Kathleen. *William Blake*. London: Thames & Hudson, 2000.

Shelley, Percy Bysshe. *A Defense of Poetry*. Originally written in 1821, first published posthumously in 1840 in *Essays, Letters from Abroad, Translations and Fragments* by Edward Moxon in London.

The Book of Job. Trans. Stephen Mitchell. New York: Harper Perennial, 1992.

Teresa of Avila. *The Interior Castle. The Complete Works of St. Teresa*. 2nd volume. Trans. and ed. E. Ellison Peers. London: Sheed & Ward, 1957.